Invited Home

Hospitality and the Heart of God

Mike Dietrich

Scripture quotations, unless otherwise noted, are from the HOLY BIBLE, NEW INTERNATIONAL VERSION. Copyright 1973, 1978, 1984 International Bible Society. Used by permission of Zondervan Bible Publishers.

Dedication

This book is dedicated to the people who have welcomed me hospitably into their lives and made a place for me to feel like I belong: Paul Hall, who first introduced me to Jesus; David Clarke, who taught me about the love, passion, and power of Jesus; Denys and Maxine Clarke who took me in as a son; Lynn and Della Berntson who did the same; Mike Dunn, Todd and Tina Dermody, and Kim and Dana Moore who have loved me like a brother; Jason Deslongchamp and Jacob Holman who are like sons to me, and welcome me into their lives as a friend and mentor; the people of Eastside Bible Church, Trinity Church, and City Life Fellowship, who have included me in countless life-giving ways in their lives; Gib Martin – my sorely-missed and dearly loved mentor, friend, confidant and spiritual dad; and my wife and sons, Becky, Jedd, and Tyler, who have teamed with me on the adventure of entertaining angels, and have attained angelic stature as a result.

INVITED HOME

Contents

INVITED HOME

I. SOMETHING MYSTERIOUS

Not only had I never been to Palo Alto California before, but I had never stayed for three weeks (yes, *three weeks*) in the home of total strangers. And yet, there I was, a recently-married 23 year-old, the guest of people I had never met, hoping for the best. Would they be friendly, or ferocious? Would they make me feel welcome and at ease, or would I feel lonely and uncomfortable and wish I was safely back home with my wife in familiar surroundings? I was definitely having second thoughts about this foray into the unknown, but such were the circumstances I had agreed to subject myself to in order to attend a pastor's conference at Peninsula Bible Church. Each attendee was assigned to stay in the home of one of the leaders in the church. In my case, the youngest daughter had gladly given up her bedroom and moved into her sister's room to make a comfortable and private place for this unknown stranger. And there we all were, Lynn and Della, and their three children Holly, Becky, and Dan, sitting around the dinner table that first night, laughing uproariously because Becky had thought my stay in her room was actually going to be three MONTHS, rather than three weeks. This new revelation understandably produced in her a certain relief.

The dinner that night, some 40 years ago, was a foretaste of something transcendent – a rare and wonderful experience that has powerfully influenced my life ever since. The meal was simple and delicious, but made even more memorable by the relaxed conversation and interaction in which all five of my hosts somehow managed to make me feel welcomed, valued, at ease – part of the family. But that same meal was interrupted at least two or three times by knocks at the door as friends, and friends of friends, were welcomed and invited to stay and share in our dinner. As the crowd kept getting bigger the table was extended and chairs were added. Food seemed to miraculously multiply to meet the demand, and the inclusion of each new guest increased the sense of welcome and celebration, and, counter-intuitively, even the sense of intimacy. It was a diverse group that evening; students from Stanford, a wandering hippy or two (it was the early

70's after all), a young couple from church, a few neighbors, and the enormous family dog Brandy. Questions about each person's life were asked and answered. Everyone was treated with careful courtesy as he or she talked. We listened thoughtfully, laughed at the funny, wept at the painful, and shared words of encouragement, and ideas and insights about each person's process.

Conversation continued after dinner as we all moved into the living room and sat in comfortable chairs or on cushions on the floor - sipping coffee and eating scoops of Della's homemade apple crisp. The dialogue ranged from the silly to the serious, and finally, as it got quite late, people reluctantly took their leave, delighting in the mysterious, wonderful, special gift of that night - the gift of hospitality.

Have you ever had an experience like that? A gathering of people where the conversation was easy, spontaneous, thoughtful, interesting, enlightening, uplifting; where you felt like you belonged and were a welcome and important part of a circle of friends new and old; where barriers between people dissolved and fearful self-consciousness dissipated; where each person could give and receive, listen and contribute; where the simple joy, and delight, and surprise of unalloyed fellowship actually happened, and it was an event that you realized afterward was a rare and elusive gift that you hoped you might experience again sometime?

If you've never had such an encounter, you have missed out on the very thing we were all made for, and the thing we look forward to in its fulfillment when we get to heaven. Hospitality is the experience of being fully at home with other people in all its delight and mystery. It's the experience of real fellowship. It's the experience of love. And it's the experience made possible when a hospitable welcome is extended to anyone who will receive it.

There's something special about hospitality. It's more than just knowing how to put on a nice dinner, or having a bunch of friends over to watch the Super Bowl. In fact, maybe my three weeks in Palo Alto has already got you thinking that true hospitality involves something sacred – something that is mixed up with God, and who he is, and what he's all about. My belief is that this is emphatically the case, and I'm hoping you're curious enough about this very important subject to be interested in going on a journey with me to explore the joy, adventure, challenge, excitement, pleasure, pain, miracle, gift, and yes – *mystery*, that is hospitality...

THE HEART OF HOSPITALITY

If you're still reading, then welcome to the journey! Let's get started by taking a look at one of the most powerful stories of hospitality that has ever been written, authored by one of the great storytellers of all time – Jesus of Nazareth. The story I'm talking about is recorded in the Bible. It is a parable that Jesus told and gives us insight into what's at the heart of hospitality. In it, Jesus helps us see something true regarding how God thinks and feels about people…and not just about *nice* people, but about all of us - even the ones who are foolish, and rebellious, and sinful, and perverted, and addicted. Some of you may be very familiar with this story, and some may have never heard it before, but because it provides such a powerful insight into how God himself feels about you and me, I think it is very important to read it through, even if you've read it many times before.

> [11] Jesus continued: "There was a man who had two sons.
> [12] The younger one said to his father, 'Father, give me my share of the estate.' So he divided his property between them.
> [13] "Not long after that, the younger son got together all he had, set off for a distant country and there squandered his wealth in wild living.

¹⁴ After he had spent everything, there was a severe famine in that whole country, and he began to be in need.

¹⁵ So he went and hired himself out to a citizen of that country, who sent him to his fields to feed pigs.

¹⁶ He longed to fill his stomach with the pods that the pigs were eating, but no one gave him anything.

¹⁷ "When he came to his senses, he said, 'How many of my father's hired men have food to spare, and here I am starving to death!

¹⁸ I will set out and go back to my father and say to him: Father, I have sinned against heaven and against you.

¹⁹ I am no longer worthy to be called your son; make me like one of your hired men.'

²⁰ So he got up and went to his father. "But while he was still a long way off, his father saw him and was filled with compassion for him; he ran to his son, threw his arms around him and kissed him.

²¹ "The son said to him, 'Father, I have sinned against heaven and against you. I am no longer worthy to be called your son.'

²² "But the father said to his servants, 'Quick! Bring the best robe and put it on him. Put a ring on his finger and sandals on his feet.

²³ Bring the fattened calf and kill it. Let's have

a feast and celebrate.

²⁴ For this son of mine was dead and is alive again; he was lost and is found.' So they began to celebrate.

²⁵ "Meanwhile, the older son was in the field. When he came near the house, he heard music and dancing.

²⁶ So he called one of the servants and asked him what was going on.

²⁷ 'Your brother has come,' he replied, 'and your father has killed the fattened calf because he has him back safe and sound.'

²⁸ "The older brother became angry and refused to go in. So his father went out and pleaded with him.

²⁹ But he answered his father, 'Look! All these years I've been slaving for you and never disobeyed your orders. Yet you never gave me even a young goat so I could celebrate with my friends.

³⁰ But when this son of yours who has squandered your property with prostitutes comes home, you kill the fattened calf for him!'

³¹ "'My son,' the father said, 'you are always with me, and everything I have is yours.

³² But we had to celebrate and be glad, because this brother of yours was dead and is alive again; he was lost and is found.'" (Luke

15:11-32)

This parable is commonly known as "the parable of the Prodigal Son." It is a good description because prodigal means extravagantly wasteful, and indeed Jesus describes very clearly the **prodigality** of this young man. He was so completely self-absorbed and foolish that he was willing to reject everything he had been taught about right and wrong, and squander all his inheritance on a crazy excursion into promiscuity and drunkenness. But I like to call it "the parable of the Prodigal Son and the Prodigious Father." It's interesting to me that prodigal and prodigious come from the same root word, but have nearly opposite meanings. In this case, by contrast, the **prodigious-ness** of the father's heart toward his son is seen in the immense love and grace, manifested in the open and overflowing welcome the father displayed toward this dissolute and dissipated young man.

What we have going on here is instruction from God himself on the meaning of hospitality. Without condemnation or a stern lecture of any kind, the father welcomed his returning son with open arms - with extravagance of forgiveness and exuberance of joy. He didn't even let his son finish his groveling speech of repentance. He just threw his arms around him and shouted to everybody in his household to drop everything and fire up the barbeque for a special party. *That* is God's heart of hospitality – his open arms of welcome, ready to embrace anyone no matter their sordid past, who will simply turn from their foolishness and receive his welcome.

If you ever want to see hospitality defined and demonstrated, you need look no further than the parable of the Prodigal Son and the Prodigious Father. Hospitality, at its heart, is the expression of the heart of God who freely welcomes strangers and friends alike into his presence. Hospitality is God's delight in celebrating the value of every person, and going the extra mile to make each person see and understand that he is valued. And nothing could be more timely in our poor culture where the value of each person is so eroded. This erosion of personal value has occurred because of such abuses as easy abortion, rampant pornography, the obsessive preoccupation with wealth and appearance, (I'm nothing if I'm not skinny, beautiful, or have well defined abs), as well as the deeply ingrained concept that I am not God's special creation, but merely the product of the convergence of the impersonal, plus time, plus chance.

But God's hospitable heart stands as a bright hope against the devaluing of the human being. He has gone to great lengths to demonstrate how deeply he values you and me, and this truth is potently demonstrated in this great parable.

The story further illustrates how God values us by showing that his hospitality is not a passive thing. You will notice that the father saw his son coming "from a long way off." Why do you think that was? Because, most likely, he spent many hours on his roof looking out on the horizon in hopes that he might see his son's familiar silhouette coming his way. And once he finally did see him off in the distance, he didn't just wait for his son to arrive, but instead, eagerly ran out to embrace him. Wild horses couldn't have kept him on that roof. So a real heart of hospitality reaches out and takes the initiative to welcome people.

I've come to understand that what made that very special evening with Lynn and Della possible – as well as many other evenings during that memorable three weeks stay in Palo Alto – was that they were filled with the hospitable heart of God. As I watched them during that time I was a guest in their house, I saw that remarkable first evening at dinner as not just something which happened by chance. Lynn and Della were people who delighted in other people. They welcomed everyone into their lives. They were interested in each person's story. They were busy people, but never too busy to stop and give time and attention to someone. If their children's friends came over, they were engaged with them in conversation. If friends from church dropped by with new friends, yard work stopped, iced tea was served, and relationships were cultivated. If someone needed advice or a listening ear, Lynn and Della were there with patience and with prayer. And like the Prodigious Father, they weren't passive, but always reaching out to new people they encountered, inviting them into their home to enjoy a meal and a conversation and a laugh and a hug. Unlike the curmudgeonly and ungrateful brother in the parable, they looked for opportunities to embrace people and include them in the circle of fellowship and grace that they created wherever they went, because they knew they had something wonderful to share. They had experienced the warm welcome of God's loving hospitality in their own lives, and so were eager to share the same experience with anyone else who might be interested.

Have you ever felt that way; that as someone whom God has blessed with his love and grace and forgiveness, you wanted to share the same thing with other people? Well, that's because the love in God's heart has been infused into your heart when you believed in him. The Apostle Paul said this very thing in Romans 5:

⁵ And hope does not disappoint us, because God has poured out his love into our hearts by the Holy Spirit, whom he has given us. (Romans 5:5)

So hospitality is not something foreign to people who believe in God. If you are a Christian, you have experienced God's loving welcome – the very welcome that Jesus pictured in the parable of the Prodigal Son and the Prodigious Father. And that same love which motivated God to welcome you and me has been poured into our hearts so that we can love others in the same way, and thereby demonstrate to them what God is like. And this is very much God's desire for us. We know this because the Bible contains God's explicit mandate to "practice hospitality" (Rom.12.13); God's commendation for those who do (3 John.5); and the explanation that hospitality is a qualification for leadership in the church. (1 Tim.3.2; Titus 1.8). We will discuss this further in a later chapter, but for now I just want you to see that God has given us the resources we need to live hospitably in relationship to others.

By the way, if you're not someone who believes in Jesus, you're still not excluded from the wonderful experience of God's hospitable heart - but more on that later.

In the meantime, what an adventure God has offered us! He has invited and authorized us to be his ambassadors by showing hospitality to everyone he brings our way. He has summoned us to travel with people – as J.R.R. Tolkien would say – on an "unexpected journey." It's a journey laced with excitement, joy, and yes – even some danger – as we risk ourselves to uncover the treasures hidden within the lives of folks who are seeking a safe and secure place in the world to call home. Now I know to some of us, that is a frightening and/or burdensome proposition. Maybe you're worried that you just don't have anything worthwhile to give, or that it's too much work, or too expensive, or too demanding, or that you're too poor, or too busy, or that you just don't know how. But if you have some of those reservations, let me urge you to read on, because I think you will see that hospitality is anything but a loathsome task. In fact, I think you will see it's an invitation to experience the joy and wonder of that first night at Lynn and Della's. And to help you, we will look at some simple and basic things about hospitality that you can do, which will serve to dissipate those reservations. But ultimately hospitality is something that God himself is eager to shape in you, and he is certainly up to the task - it's just a matter of having an open heart and mind.

15

What do you think? Can you embrace this? Are you interested in the journey? Well, I hope you'll say yes, because there are rare and wonderful things to discover about yourself and about God as we explore the hidden treasure of this nearly lost gift.

II. HOSPITALITY AND HOME

I have built two houses with my own hands, and building is a very creative work. You first must come up with a design. Then you have to find a place for this house to exist. Additionally, you have to procure materials that the house will be made of. And finally you must shape and manipulate and fasten those materials together into a form that - more or less - manifests in a physical way the idea you started with. But even before all that, you must have a *reason* to build a house. And for me and my wife, that reason was always HOSPITALITY.

Now that may seem like a strange reason to build a house, but think about it with me for a minute. We needed a place to *be*. We needed something that would shelter us from the weather, give us a place to eat, sleep, raise children, interact with friends, study, create, relax; a place to accommodate the various activities that make up a life. In other words, we needed a place in the world that would welcome us by providing the necessary environment to function in life. So, it was out of a desire to provide a welcoming place for my wife and my children and my friends and acquaintances that I built our house. And isn't that really what hospitality is? It's all about welcoming people, and giving them a place to belong. And in order to welcome someone, you need to create a welcoming environment.

So maybe hospitality is not so strange a reason, after all, for building a house. And maybe you can see, by the same token, that neither is it a strange reason for God to create the universe. In fact, when you think about it, the first action by God reported in the Bible is a wonderful demonstration of the hospitable heart of God. "In the beginning, God created the heavens and the earth." (Genesis 1.1) As we read the Genesis account, it is obvious that man was not an afterthought when God created the universe, but the very reason that he went to all the trouble. In his wisdom and love God decided to create a being in his image and likeness. And in doing so he went to unfathomable lengths to create a hospitable environment of infinite potentialities, where man could live creatively and intimately with God, other men, and his world. God prepared a place for man to happily and fruitfully *be*. Out of chaos he produced order and beauty, separating light from darkness and water from dry land; putting lights in the sky and plants and animals on the ground; providing food to eat, and creative things to do. God even planted a splendid garden for Adam and Eve to live in as their home, with breathtaking trees and awe-inspiring water works. I imagine terraces planted with exotic flowers and fruits, and jewel-colored birds flitting among branches and twittering beautiful music. I think there must have been strangely wonderful animals roaming contentedly. In my mind's eye I see meandering streams and exuberant waterfalls, pools and grottos and fountains large and small; places of beauty and shelter to bathe, and rest, and quench the thirst. And I see all these as expressions of the hospitable heart of God as he welcomed man into existence by creating for us this magnificent place to live.

Well, all this tells us something wonderful about hospitality, doesn't it? The very act of creating the universe was God being hospitable to man. And having built houses myself I can see how this works. Because I had a wife and children who I loved and cherished and wanted to provide for, I was excited about creating a place to welcome them. I thought long and hard about what kind of environment would inspire them, protect them, enhance their lives and meet their needs. I wanted it to be beautiful, and useful, and to bless their lives and enable their potential. I wanted it to be a place where they felt safe and loved. And I also wanted it to be a place where we could welcome others.

Now if this is true about a very imperfect husband and father, how much more is it true about God! You may not have thought this before, but can you see how God's love toward man is magnificently revealed in his creation of the universe? Can you see how, when God created the heavens and the earth, it was and is a manifestation of his prodigious hospitality toward us?

So from the very beginning of history God's character is revealed as brimming with hospitality. He is a God who went to great lengths to create a welcoming and nurturing place for us to come into existence and inhabit. He spent five of the six days of creation preparing an environment for us to be at home in.

But, if you look closely at the Bible, you can see how God's hospitable character is manifested with the same magnificence at the very end of history as well. In (John 14.1-3) Jesus explains that he is just as interested in preparing a place for us to call home - a place where he can welcome us and nurture us and fellowship with us - for the rest of eternity when history as we know it comes to an end - as he was when history began. Look at what Jesus said:

> "Do not let your hearts be troubled. Trust in God; trust also in me. In my Father's house are many rooms; if it were not so, I would have told you. I am going there to prepare a place for you. And if I go and prepare a place for you, I will come back and take you to be with me that you also may be where I am."
> (John 14:1-3)

Here Jesus is describing part of what he will be doing in the interim between now and his return at the end of this present age. He is saying that after he rose from the dead and ascended into heaven he would be preparing a special place for each one of us to be at home with him.

When I built our first house it was a labor of love. At times it was cold, and miserable, and back-breaking labor. You should never try to build a house in Seattle in the winter. We had actually planned to build it in the summer, but Seattle-area cities have draconian laws and regulations that must be complied with before any dirt is shoveled and any nail is hammered. So cold winter rain dripped down my back, and snow made the roof slippery, and numb fingers were clumsily hit by many a hammer, as our summer start-building date gave way to late autumn, and the building process continued through the dead of winter.

And yet, as miserable as it sometimes was, I was still excited to go to the work site every day and work and watch as a home slowly took shape. And as I look back at it I think it was a kind of excitement born of the anticipation that one day soon the preparation would be done and I would be able to welcome my family into our home where we would be able to live happily and creatively together.

And I think this is the very thing that is going on with Jesus in John 14. I believe this passage conveys Jesus' sense of joy and anticipation as he awaits the moment when he will welcome us into the special home he has thoughtfully designed for each one of us – and where that longing for home we all experience will be completely fulfilled in the ultimate expression of God's hospitality. As special as our first little house was, it will be nothing compared to the one Jesus is preparing for us now. The Scripture hints at it with these words:

> "No eye has seen, no ear has heard, no mind has conceived what God has prepared for those who love him." (1 Corinthians 2:9)

So what we can see is that history is book-ended with extravagant acts of hospitality by God toward man. From the very beginning when God created the heavens and the earth to welcome us into history, to the very end where Jesus has created a special place in God's "house" to welcome us out of history and into eternity, God's hospitable heart has been moved to invite us to share in his life, his love, his purposes, and most of all in fellowship with him.

Unfortunately some people have a very different view of God – if not intellectually, at least emotionally. Many people see or feel about God as if he is distant, stern, cold, judgmental and prickly. They sometimes think of God as a great cosmic killjoy leaning down over the parapets of heaven and shouting "Cut that out!"…that he is aloof and distant from men and women and would prefer to keep it that way. But I'm hoping, if you're one of those people, that these passages from the Bible will help you see him differently and more accurately.

The Bible is, after all, God's revelation of himself, and it shows us that God's deepest desire is to welcome us with joy and celebration into his presence, and that he has made this possible through the work of Jesus on the cross. You may be very familiar with this truth about Jesus and the cross, or it may be new to you. But either way, it is the most wonderful truth - the best news that men and women could ever hear - so I want to explain it in more detail. However in this case, I think we'll save the best for last. (The last chapter, that is.) For now I just want you to see that hospitality is the practical manifestation of what people call the "grace" of God, and in many ways gives us the truest view of how God feels and acts toward you and me, always at work to provide us a place to be at home, both in the living of our lives, and in an intimate relationship with him.

So let's explore the idea of "home" a little further in the next chapter, because it not only helps us to understand something about God, but also something about ourselves. It's a powerful longing we all share in common. You may not have ever identified it; you may only be vaguely aware of it; but I think as we explore it you will agree that deep within your soul there is a force that works upon you and calls you into action, and that you may never have seen until now as something intrinsic to being the person that you are. It's what I call THE LONGING FOR HOME.

III. THE LONGING FOR HOME

Not everyone has built a house like I did - in fact most people don't. But we can all identify with the instinct. We all need a place to be "at home." And of course, as we've seen, the need is very practical. We need shelter from the cold; a place to eat, sleep, and live. We all need a space that is ours to occupy - a place to go after work, or to simply *be* when we're not doing anything in particular. In fact, this is why being homeless is such a violation of our humanity; because when I'm homeless, I don't have a place where I'm welcome to simply exist, apart from anything I do. A homeless person has to exist unwelcome and uninvited in a hostile environment. He doesn't fit anywhere. He has no place to call his own - no place he has a right to occupy without being an inconvenience, a burden, or a trespasser – no place where he belongs.

Looking at the subject from this very fundamental point of view helps us see how universal and basic the need for home is. And we can see that it's not simply a need for shelter. Even more fundamentally, it is the need for a space that corresponds to the fact that I exist. A home makes me feel that I not only have the right to exist, but that I'm actually welcome in the world. So, returning again to the Genesis account, Adam and Eve were at home in the world because God made them a specific place that was their own within that world, the Garden of Eden. So even though it was their mandate to fill the earth and subdue it, I imagine that no matter how far out into the world they ventured, they always returned home to Eden where they felt they most belonged. It was in Eden that things were most familiar, and where Adam and Eve most fully expressed their own creativity lived out in harmony with God who taught them and encouraged them. As a result, I imagine it was there that they felt most welcome in the world, even though the world was not the hostile place it now is. And this must be the case simply because God went to the trouble to make Eden for Adam and Eve.

My point is that since God made a special place for Adam and Eve - that out of the whole wide world he created Eden as their home - then it must be because "home" corresponds to something in our nature. And since we are created in the image of God, that "something" in our nature is a reflection of something in God himself.

So what is that thing in the very personality of God that is all about home? Isn't it that, within the godhead (Father, Son, and Holy Spirit), there is unbroken love, perfect fellowship, mutual respect, absolute welcome, complete belonging, utter familiarity, unending curiosity, total knowing and being known, and a resultant absolute joy, with no hint of threat, danger, misunderstanding, discomfort, jealousy, dysfunction, want, or lack of any kind? And aren't these the very words that come to mind when asked to describe what it means for you to feel at home? So my conclusion is that, being made in the image of God, home is built into our very nature. And further, that ever since the fall, just as Adam and Eve were expelled from their home in the Garden of Eden, so we have lost our at-home-ness with God, with one another, and with our environment. In fact I might even go so far as to say that one of man's deepest and most fundamental wounds is his loss of home. We are, in a sense, homeless in the universe, and we know instinctively that something is therefore amiss. The alienation we feel is the result of this homelessness and has created in us a deep longing for home.

Some of our great literature captures this longing. You'll know what I mean if you've read one of my favorite authors, J.R.R. Tolkien. For instance, in Tolkien's "The Hobbit" you are invited into wonderful places that evoke the sense of home that I'm talking about. In fact, Tolkien's writing sharpens my longing for home as he describes such places as Bilbo's hobbit house.

> "In a hole in the ground there lived a hobbit. Not a nasty, dirty, wet hole, filled with the ends of worms and an oozy smell, nor yet a dry, bare, sandy hole with nothing in it to sit down on or to eat: it was a hobbit-hole, and that means comfort." (The Hobbit, JRR Tolkien, The Easton Press, Norwalk Ct., P.9)

With its round, green-painted door (or was it yellow?), its cozy rooms with glowing fireplaces, its larders filled with delicious things to eat, (meat pies and sausages and hams, fresh-baked bread and just-churned butter, an abundance of pickles and jams and "put up" fruits and vegetables, and ale and beer - well, you get the picture) as well as the comings and goings of all kinds of interesting and fascinating friends and acquaintances - reading about this hobbit-hole made me long to be there because I knew I would feel very much at home there.

In the same book there's the Last Homely House - a

magical place of comfort and safety where the Elves lived. And then there's the home of Beorn - a long, low, widely porched, welcoming house of logs (if I remember correctly) deep within a mysterious and dangerous forest. It had very large rooms and very high ceilings and an enormous fire giving warmth and light to a wonderful feast set at a long sturdy rustic table. Oh, and the bedrooms! Great squishy comfortable mattresses that felt like you were sleeping on a cloud, and warm soft blankets and crisp white sheets that smelled like lavender and the sea. (Or at least, that's how I remember it. If you go back and read it, it might turn out to be somewhat different, but I'm not going to wreck my memory of it with the facts!) Nevertheless, irrespective of the accuracy of my memory, it was an oasis of shelter and safety and sustenance and rest in the middle of a hostile environment - and I felt what a joy and privilege it was for the hobbit and his companions to be guests there. And again, it made me long for home - a place like it that was safe, sturdy, comfortable, and familiar.

Do these stories do the same thing to you that they do to me? Maybe for some of you at least, they do. But for those of you who think I'm just a little whacky there are other hints about this interior longing for home that I believe we all have. There's that nesting instinct that many women feel when they're about to have a baby. And what about the instinct that most men have to be a provider for their family? These are instincts centered in the need and longing for home.

And in the Bible we see God himself taking this instinct very seriously. Not only did he create, as we've already seen, a planet and a garden for Adam and Eve so they would have their own home, but he also went to a great deal of trouble later on to create a special place that His Chosen People could call home. He promised Abraham, Moses, and others that he would give his people a land of their own, full of abundant resources, where there would be no want and in which they would dwell securely. Each person would have his own property, and a house to live in, and a vine and a fig tree, and God would live with them there in intimate fellowship. In other words, each person would have food and shelter and would lack nothing of life's necessities, including a close and vital relationship with God himself. (See Exodus.3.8; Ezekiel 28.26; 1 Kings 4.25) In short, their need and longing for home would be fulfilled, at least to some significant extent.

So what has this longing for home got to do with hospitality? The two are like mirror images. The longing for home is the need, and hospitality is the fulfillment of that need. When we are hospitable toward someone, what we are doing is, in one way or another, providing a home for that person. That is what hospitality actually is. I'm practicing hospitality when I create a welcome place in my life for someone else. Whether it is just eye contact and a smile as I pass a stranger in the grocery store, or taking the time to chat with someone while waiting in line, I'm practicing hospitality. I'm saying "Hi, come on in…make yourself at home." When I sit at Starbucks with a friend old or new, and listen to their story and ask them questions about themselves, I'm practicing hospitality. I'm saying there's room in my heart and my life for you, and you're welcome there. And of course, it goes both ways. When I share my own life transparently and vulnerably with someone else I'm being hospitable as well. I'm saying "Come in and see my life's living room, and study, and kitchen. Sit on my furniture and share it with me." That's hospitality.

Hospitality, then, is the restoration - not perfectly in this life, but substantially - of the at-home-ness that God intended for us to experience in life. Hospitality is leaving the hostile environment of alienation, and being welcomed into reconciled relationships. When hospitality is exercised it changes a person's status from stranger to welcome family member. In fact, being hospitable is so important and compelling that when it is practiced it actually causes the Kingdom of God to break into this present life. When you are hospitable to someone you are giving that person a taste of heaven; you are introducing them to God's very purpose for their lives - to find their way back home again.

So, in the next chapter, let's look at the amazing, powerful, transforming impact hospitality can have on another person, or group of people, or even a whole culture.

IV. The Hospitable Healer

It's fascinating to read in the Bible about how Jesus approached people. You will notice that his posture toward people was almost always one of openness and welcome. Look, for example, at Jesus' interaction with a little man named Zacchaeus.

> 1 Jesus entered Jericho and was passing through. 2 A man was there by the name of Zacchaeus; he was a chief tax collector and was wealthy. 3 He wanted to see who Jesus was, but being a short man he could not, because of the crowd. 4 So he ran ahead and climbed a sycamore-fig tree to see him, since Jesus was coming that way. 5 When Jesus reached the spot, he looked up and said to him, "Zacchaeus, come down immediately. I must stay at your house today." 6 So he came

down at once and welcomed him gladly. 7 All the people saw this and began to mutter, "He has gone to be the guest of a 'sinner.'" 8 But Zacchaeus stood up and said to the Lord, "Look, Lord! Here and now I give half of my possessions to the poor, and if I have cheated anybody out of anything, I will pay back four times the amount." 9 Jesus said to him, "Today salvation has come to this house, because this man, too, is a son of Abraham. 10 For the Son of Man came to seek and to save what was lost." (Luke 19:1-10)

From Luke's description of this event we know several things about this interesting man. He was a chief tax collector, he was wealthy, he was short, and he was so curious about Jesus that he was willing to put himself through the indignity of climbing a tree in order to get a view of him.

Now in Jesus' day, a chief tax collector was not the most popular guy in town. In fact they were a despised class of Jews who collected duties and tolls on behalf of the hated Roman government. But to add insult to injury, they added an additional amount to the tax burden for their own profit. It was a kind of extortion that was viewed by the Jews as treasonous politically, and blasphemous religiously. And it was on this basis that Zacchaeus had become a wealthy man, and was definitely persona non grata as far as the religious establishment was concerned. He clearly was a kind of moral and ethical low-life, and as a result was an outcast from his own people. He was viewed as without hope and without God in the world - emphatically not at home in the Jewish culture.

And yet, he had heard about Jesus, and somehow was so attracted by what he heard that he went to great lengths just to get a view of him as he passed by in the crowd. And when Jesus saw him up in the tree, and invited himself to dinner at Zacchaeus' house, I imagine Zacchaeus was just as surprised by the invitation as the religious crowd was indignant.

But at what were they indignant? Wasn't it indignation at the hospitality of God? Wasn't it a self-righteous disdain at a God who openly welcomes anyone who's interested in Jesus, to be at home in his presence?

Now you may be thinking that Jesus wasn't being hospitable so much as he was being presumptuous by inviting himself to dinner at Zacchaeus' house. But remember, hospitality is always a two-way proposition. It is hospitable to open your home to someone, but it is just as hospitable to accept the invitation. Hospitality can't come to fruition without both initiative and response. Our efforts at hospitality can be frustrated if people refuse our welcome. So Jesus extended his welcome, and his embrace, and his inclusion to Zacchaeus by asking Zacchaeus to welcome him. "I must stay at your house today." It's the same idea expressed by Jesus in (Rev.3.20); "Behold I stand at the door and knock. If anyone hears my voice and opens the door, I will come in to him, and dine with him, and he with me." And of course Zacchaeus responded eagerly and with great delight. "So he came down at once and welcomed him gladly."

So Jesus' encounter with Zacchaeus is another beautiful example of the unencumbered hospitality of God toward a fallen and sinful man. It is another window into the heart of God who openly, eagerly, and with delight welcomes us into fellowship with him regardless of our religious respectability - if we simply show any kind of interest in Jesus.

But additionally, one of the wonderful things to see from this encounter is what God's hospitality did to Zacchaeus. As the on-looking crowd muttered at the scandal of Jesus associating with a "sinner," Zacchaeus spontaneously, on the spot, turned away from the life of greed and extortion that had consumed him. "Look, Lord! Here and now I give half of my possessions to the poor, and if I have cheated anybody out of anything, I will pay back four times the amount." The hospitality of God, freely extended to Zacchaeus, radically re-oriented him - changed his values - changed his heart. In fact, wasn't the powerful force that attracted Zacchaeus to Jesus - his open welcome to the least, last, and lost - wasn't that the very thing that transformed Zacchaeus into someone entirely new?

My guess is that Zacchaeus very much viewed himself in the same way that the crowd around him did. He probably shared their disdain of his life style but was entrenched, trapped, and addicted to his own wealth. I imagine he had many regrets about his past choices and was probably full of self-loathing. Maybe even the fact that he was short contributed to his woundedness and gave him a chip on his shoulder, and in order to be able to live with himself he cultivated a cynicism and sarcasm toward life and especially toward God.

And then suddenly, into the life of this hopeless and hurting man came Jesus, the son of God, inviting himself to dinner at Zacchaeus' house! In Jesus, God was contradicting all of Zacchaeus' presuppositions. Jesus' hospitality was showing Zacchaeus that he had worth - that he was valuable to God. Jesus' welcome was giving Zacchaeus hope that maybe God didn't hate him, but loved him. Jesus' invitation was opening Zacchaeus' heart to the idea that his life could have meaning and purpose. And all this grace made it possible for Zacchaeus to let go of the idols of wealth and position that made him a user of people, and a violator of his own conscience. The hospitality of God can heal the heart of man. In fact, the very word "hospitality" is related to the word "hospital." Just as in a hospital, when we experience hospitality we are nurtured, strengthened, and served. As with a hospital, hospitality helps others find physical, spiritual, and emotional help, and the effect on people is that they are healthier and more whole as a result.

If you look at the many people that Jesus healed from the perspective of hospitality, you will see this same welcoming inclusion - this invitation to be at home with God - in virtually every example. For instance, in (Luke 5.12) a leper came to Jesus and begged him saying "Lord, if you are willing you can make me clean." And Jesus responded with the most extraordinary act of hospitality. He didn't heal him from a distance in order to keep himself uncontaminated by this awful disease. Instead, the Bible says, "He reached out and TOUCHED him and said 'I am willing; be cleansed.' And immediately the leprosy left him." Jesus invited the leper into his life, and extended to him the welcoming hospitality of God by actually touching him. This was an unthinkable act for a rabbi, or anyone else for that matter, in Jesus' day. The leper was healed physically of his terrible, debilitating disease. But don't you think, in addition, that there was an internal healing of this poor, outcast, despised man by virtue of the fact that Jesus touched him? This leper had probably not felt a human touch for years - maybe decades. But now God, in the person of Jesus, said in effect "you are not unclean to me - you are not outcast from me - I welcome you - I love you - I embrace you, body, soul, and spirit." In a wonderful demonstration of God's hospitable encirclement, this leper was healed from his terrible disease, and was made to see himself as valuable and welcome and at home with God.

We see the same healing power of hospitality in Jesus' encounter with all the people who came to him in need of God's help; the woman at the well, (Jn.4.1-42); the woman caught in adultery, (Jn.8.1-11); the paralytic who was let down through the roof, (Lk.5.17-26); the servant of the Roman official, (Lk.7.1-10); the woman who couldn't stop bleeding, (Mt.9.20-21); the healing of blind Bartimaeus, (Mk.10.46-52); the man with the crippled hand, (Mk.3.1-6); the woman who couldn't stand up straight, (Lk.13.10-17); etc. etc. Some, but not all of them were physical healings. Yet all were powerful demonstrations of healing the deep wounds of men and women who were homeless in life because of the hostile environment of fallen-ness that makes us all feel like outcasts in the world. What we see from these examples is that Jesus invites us *all* to dine with him. None of us need ever again be tortured by the isolation of our own brokenness, because God is hospitable to the broken.

Have you ever experienced this kind of hospitality from Jesus? I can tell you that for me, growing up in a family unfamiliar with the Christian faith, a hospitable God was never part of my thinking or experience of life. My parents were divorced when I was eight, and the security of a mom and dad who loved each other and were committed to nurturing a family was not part of the vocabulary of my youth. I can also tell you that as a high schooler in the late '60s, when friends returned from the jungles of Viet Nam in flag-draped boxes, and when so many around me were experimenting with drugs and sex and Timothy Leary's counsel to "tune in, turn on, and drop out", I was feeling very much the lack of an anchor in life. Nothing felt secure or certain. Life was laced with a sense of meaninglessness, and I was hungry emotionally and spiritually, for a place to call home.

My first encounter with the welcoming, hospitable nature of Jesus came in the form of a young man named Paul. On the first day of my first class, in my first year of college, while waiting in the hallway for our English professor to finish his cigarette before opening the classroom door, I encountered Paul. He was a clean-cut kid with a soft Texas accent, a ready smile, a friendly manner, and a clear countenance that said "welcome into my life." We struck up a conversation, and over the next few weeks became good friends.

Now I must tell you, I don't think I had ever met a more welcoming and friendly guy. There was just something about him - easy going, not a touch of cynicism, considerate to a fault. He was fun-loving, had a great sense of humor, and was curious about my life - what made me tick - what was important to me. He was devoted to his girlfriend, but always had time for other people as well. It was almost as if this guy was too good to be true. I was kind of waiting for the other shoe to drop - like maybe in his other life he was really a serial killer or something. So when the other shoe did drop, it was not at all what I expected.

Paul showed up one day for English class, and we were waiting in the hall as usual for the prof to finish his cigarette. As we were standing there talking I noticed a little button pinned to his shirt that had some kind of statement about Jesus on it.

"Oh no," I thought to myself, "Paul is one of those Jesus guys!" I wasn't hostile to Jesus, but kind of mystified by him, and as a result, religious people made me rather nervous. But Paul didn't make me nervous, and he was one of those religious guys, so I kind of relaxed about it and did my best to ignore it. Some weeks later my curiosity got the best of me however, and I started asking him about his faith. He was able to explain to me very simply that Jesus was alive and real, and that he was inviting me into a relationship with him. But as I look back on it now, what so powerfully opened my heart to the loving welcome of Jesus, and what dissipated my fear about things "religious", was the welcoming and hospitable heart of Jesus manifested through my friend Paul.

Here was a guy who made me feel at home around him. He accepted me just like I was, and loved me like a friend. He cared about people in a way that caused him to be a thoughtful listener and an encourager. Paul made you feel like you had value, and there was nothing you had to do to earn his approval - it was just there - a free gift. His life was an open invitation to friendship - hospitality incarnate. And as with Zacchaeus and the leper, this hospitality began a work of healing in my life by helping me start to find my way back home. Paul's hospitable welcome as a friend, coupled with his faith, opened my heart to the possibility that there might be a God who created me, loves me, and has a plan for my life. And that work of healing has been helped along by many other acts of welcoming and acceptance by many other people who, just like Paul, powerfully manifested the love and grace of God by practicing hospitality in my life.

Can you see why God doesn't call us to practice religion, but does call us to "practice hospitality"? (1Pet.4.9) Because as his ambassadors to wounded, outcast, broken men and women, we are, through hospitality, carrying on the same healing ministry that Jesus demonstrated. By welcoming others into our lives and into our homes we are applying the healing balm of God to the central woundedness of man.

SPECIAL NOTE: I feel like it's important to add at this point that if you are reading this and have never discovered this hospitable God who I'm talking about, and you're curious about a relationship with him, you might want to skip to the last chapter for a moment. God is eager to welcome you into a relationship with him, and it's not a vague or incomprehensible process. In that chapter I try to clarify, in a simple way, how to respond to the invitation of Jesus to "dine with him." But if you do go to that chapter, make sure to come back here and read on…because there is more to learn about the great adventure of hospitality, and God wants to include you in that adventure.

V. THE GENEROSITY OF HOSPITALITY

As I've pondered and studied and eagerly soaked up God's hospitality in my life, I've noticed that a quality embedded in the hospitality of God is the generosity of God. If you think back over everything we've looked at so far, it is easy to see that when hospitality is expressed it is always accompanied by generosity. The two are really inseparable. God's generosity is always displayed in his hospitality. The Bible gives us poignant insight into the relationship between generosity and hospitality as it records, in 1 Samuel 25, events around a greedy fool named Nabal. You may think it rather harsh to describe anyone in that way, but when you hear what happened you will see I'm not being harsh, but simply following the Biblical example.

The context of David's encounter with Nabal is that God had decided to make David king of Israel in Saul's place, because Saul had proven to be rebellious and disobedient to God. But Saul wasn't simply going to step aside as king. He was determined to jealously guard his own power and prestige at any cost which, as you can imagine, made David's life very difficult. Because David knew that God had chosen him to be the new king, he was determined to wait for God to deal with Saul rather than to do something of his own making, even though Saul was trying to kill him. So David had taken to hiding in the wilderness with a group of several hundred men who followed him because they knew God had chosen him as king. There in the wilderness they survived by living in caves, hunting whatever game they could find, and gratefully accepting the generosity of property owners and farmers who lived nearby.

It was in this circumstance that David encountered a very wealthy man named Nabal, and his beautiful wife Abigail. David and his men were in need of food, and when David heard that Nabal was in the area he sent ten young men to ask if Nabal would show him favor and give them whatever extra food he could spare. David also told the messengers to remind Nabal that when his shepherds had encountered David and his men in the wilderness they were well treated; that in fact, David and his men had actually acted as protectors of Nabal's possessions, watching over his property so that nothing of theirs was taken. David was more or less saying "Look Nabal, we're not a band of hoodlums, we're honorable men who trust in God, but we're experiencing hard times at the moment. I treated your men and property well, protecting them in the desert against bandits and marauders, so I'm asking you to be gracious to me and my men by sharing with us a little out of your great wealth."

Here is what the Bible records as Nabal's response:

> Nabal answered David's servants, "Who is this David? And who is this son of Jesse? Many servants are breaking away from their masters these days. Why should I take my bread and water, and the meat I have slaughtered for my shearers, and give it to men coming from who knows where?" (1 Sam.25.10-11)

Now, in the first place, this was an egregious violation of desert etiquette. It was customary in David's time and culture for hospitality to be extended to anyone in need who asked for help, as long as they showed a commitment to not harm the host. So this was not just a simple "No" from Nabal. It was a slap in the face, a serious insult, a breach of customary consideration in David and Nabal's culture even if David had not been gracious to Nabal. But because, additionally, David had been an un-asked for benefactor to Nabal, it was a compounded insult.

So here is a man who stands in sharp contrast to the spirit of hospitality that we have seen demonstrated by God. Nabal was a man of great wealth, owning property and thousands of sheep and goats, with many servants and people under his employ. And yet he was a man full of greed. With all the abundance he enjoyed he would not share a small portion of it with people in need who had treated him with honor and respect. And we can see by his reaction to David that a greedy man is an inhospitable man. He didn't welcome David's men, inviting them to stay and rest and enjoy the shelter and blessing of his abundance. Instead, his greed resulted in a closed heart, a closed door, and ultimately a life closed off from the joy and freedom of new friends, new opportunities, broadened horizons, unexpected blessings, a deepened soul, an expanded spirit. His greed deadened and shrank his life, and redounded negatively to all those around him. People like Nabal who are trapped in their own greed can even provoke anger and hatred and violence in those they interact with.   Look, for example, at how David responded.

> ... "It's been useless – all my watching over this fellow's property in the desert so that nothing of his was missing. He has paid me back evil for good. May God deal with David, be it ever so severely, if by morning I leave alive one male of all who belong to him!" (1Sam.25.21-22)

David's response was certainly not a godly one. He reacted in anger and wanted vengeance. He was determined to actually kill Nabal and all of his male servants because of Nabal's mean, inconsiderate, inhospitable and greedy refusal of any help to David. But the point is that this is what greed can produce in life. It closes off relationships, it cuts hurtfully into people's hearts, it alienates and separates and wounds, and it kills any chance for hospitality to emerge and do is gracious and powerful work among people.

Fortunately for David, Nabal was married to a remarkable woman named Abigail, and because of her generous hospitality she was able to rescue David from his hot-headed response, and spare Nabal's household from the terrible violence and slaughter that David had sworn to.

The Bible records that as soon as Abigail heard about Nabal's foolishness she lost no time in taking decisive action. She gathered two hundred loaves of bread, two skins of wine, five dressed sheep, five seahs of roasted grain, a hundred cakes of raisins and two hundred cakes of pressed figs, and loaded them on donkeys. She intercepted David and his men on their way to destroy Nabal's household, hopped down from her donkey, bowed down to David with her face to the ground, and gave one of the most remarkable speeches ever recorded. Here is an excerpt:

> My lord, let the blame be on me alone. Please let your servant speak to you; hear what your servant has to say. May my lord pay no attention to that wicked man Nabal. He is just like his name – his name is Fool, and folly goes with him. But as for me, your servant, I did not see the men my master sent. Now since the Lord has kept you, my master, from bloodshed and from avenging yourself with your own hands, as surely as the Lord lives and as you live, may your enemies and all who intend to harm my master be like Nabal. And let this gift, which your servant has brought to my master, be given to the men who follow you. Please forgive your servants offense, for the Lord will certainly make a lasting dynasty

for my master, because he fights the Lord's battles. (1Sam.25.24-28a)

Wow. Here is a woman who understands something about generosity, about the power of hospitality, and about how a humble and kind word can turn away wrath. Her words alone may not have been enough; but those words accompanied by her generous act of hospitality, opening her heart to David and giving extravagantly to his need, caused David to snap out of his rage and reign in his indignation and listen to a word of truth delivered with courage and humility. Listen to David's response:

> Praise be to the Lord, the God of Israel, who has sent you today to meet me. May you be blessed for your good judgment and for keeping me from bloodshed this day and from avenging myself with my own hands. Otherwise, as surely as the Lord, the God of Israel, lives, who has kept me from harming you, if you had not come quickly to meet me, not one male belonging to Nabal would have been left alive. Then David accepted from her hand what she had brought him and said, "Go home in peace. I have heard your words and granted your request." (1Sam.25.32-35)

This very poignant story illustrates with crystal clarity the important relationship between generosity and hospitality. We can see from Nabal and Abigail's example that a greedy person is never a hospitable person, and a generous person almost always is. It shows us the damage that greed can do in an individual, and among a community of people. Nabal's greed made him a fool, and his foolishness manifested itself in an inhospitable spirit that offended and created serious conflict. It always produces death rather than life, and in Nabal's case actually resulted in his physical death, as the narrative explains:

> When Abigail went to Nabal, he was in the house holding a banquet like that of a king. He was in high spirits and very drunk. So she told him nothing until daybreak. Then in the morning, when Nabal was sober, his wife told him all these things, and his heart failed him and he became like a stone. About ten days later, the Lord struck Nabal and he died. (1Sam.25.36-38)

Isn't it incredible that here is a man who was so controlled by greed that when he heard his wife had been generous with his possessions he virtually turned to stone and ultimately died. Nabal's heart was already stony because of his love of things, but when he found that some of his things had been generously given away, it so violated his self-absorption that it caused him to implode. This is the very thing that Jesus said would happen to those who greedily grasp things to themselves.

> [33] Whoever tries to keep his life will lose it, and whoever loses his life will preserve it. (Luke 17:33)

Isn't this exactly what happened to Nabal? Rather than entrusting himself to God for his protection and to meet his needs, he trusted in his wealth. And since his wealth is what made him feel secure, he had to cling tight-fistedly to every bit of it. But in Luke 17 Jesus tries to help us see that the result of this clinging effort to make our lives secure actually results in the opposite, and the experience of Nabal shows how this works. And yet in contrast, Abigail's generosity produced in and through her the very opposite effect. She was willing to "lose her life" by being eager to act hospitably toward David and giving generously to his need. The result was, exactly as Jesus taught, that her life was preserved. Her generous and hospitable actions produced reconciliation and healing, saved many lives, and kept David from serious sin. And not incidentally, Abigail was rewarded by being freed from a miserable marriage to a terrible man, and becoming the wife of this promising young soldier who was about to become king of Israel.

The way the story of Nabal impacts me in terms of hospitality is that at times I hesitate to be hospitable, because hospitality can be costly. It can be expensive in terms of food. Usually I expect to spend at least $50 - $100 when we have guests to dinner. It can be expensive in terms of wear and tear on my home. Dishes get broken, wine gets spilled, carpets and upholstery get dirty, furniture gets dented or scratched. And it can be expensive in the giving of my time and energy. It can take many hours of thoughtful planning and more hours of work to treat my guests with the care and love that my heart wants to share with them – from planning a menu, to shopping for food, to making the house presentable, to setting the table, to actually doing the cooking. And then it takes energy and focus to actually be present to my guests – engaging them in conversation, listening to their stories, honoring their lives. Costly indeed. But Nabal warns me about the result of giving in to my selfishness. And Abigail inspires me to generosity and energy because it produces the very life that greed is trying to preserve but only destroys. My friend Dennis Peacocke, in his book <u>Doing Business God's Way</u>, puts it this way: "It is in dying to our own agenda and taking on God's agenda that I become fruitful and multiply. It is a principle of God's Cosmos that selfishness begets death, isolation, and poverty, whereas spending our lives on others is the source of life, fellowship, and multiplication."

So in order for us to be hospitable we must become generous. And one way to grow in generosity is to see clearly how generosity produces life, and how clinging greediness produces death. Allow the story of Abigail and Nabal to instruct you, warn you, and motivate you.

GENEROSITY NUANCED

Now you might think I'm finished with this subject, but you'd be wrong. (Preachers can usually find more to say on any given topic!) There is at least one other aspect of generosity and its relationship to hospitality that I want to explore with you. Look with me for a moment at a very interesting verse in the book of Proverbs that gives important instruction about the way we relate to hospitality.

> [6] Do not eat the bread of a selfish man, Or desire his delicacies;
> [7] For as he thinks within himself, so he is. He says to you, "Eat and drink!" But his heart is not with you.
> [8] You will vomit up the morsel you have eaten, And waste your compliments. (Proverbs 23:6-8) (NASB)

Here we see a person who was actually practicing

hospitality in some form. That is, he has opened his home to you. He has prepared a meal of "delicacies." Maybe he is under some kind of pressure, or he is trying to produce some kind of obligation in his guest. In Nabal's case, he was holding a banquet, the Bible says, "...like that of a king." (1Sam.25.36) His motivation was to impress his guests and show off his wealth. He was giving of his time and substance, but as with the selfish man in Proverbs, true hospitality is an issue of the heart, and his heart was not in it. The NLT translates the Proverbs passage this way; "They are always thinking about how much it costs." (v.7) The result is that the host is resentful and you are left cold.

So this passage gives us further insight into the generosity necessary for us to be genuinely hospitable. I think it will enhance the quality of our hospitality to learn from this passage that there are two different kinds of generosity. We'll call it the difference between the generosity of GIVING, and the generosity of SHARING. The host in Proverbs gave of his food, but didn't share from his heart. A way to illustrate the difference is simply this: It is one thing to *give* you my TV, and it is quite another thing to *share* with you my TV. One is being generous with my *things*, the other is being generous with my *self*. Both are good, but giving is one step removed from sharing in terms of generosity.

Psychologists have shown that one of the biggest wounds a person can suffer is produced by an absent father. An absent father can give a lot of stuff to his children – money, toys, food, clothing, shelter…all important and good things. But the most important thing is withheld…his very SELF; his time, attention, thought, creativity, his actual presence with his children. This is the generosity of giving, but not of sharing. One is good, the other is better. Both are important aspects of hospitality, but sharing really contains more of the heart of hospitality. If I give without sharing I haven't been fully hospitable because I have withheld myself – have somehow remained aloof.

The thing that was lost at the Fall was not just a place. Adam and Eve were not just expelled from the Garden of Eden, but they were cut off from God's very presence. ("Your sins have separated you from your God.") (Isa.59.2) So the loss of home that we looked at earlier was not just alienation from a place, but from the person who made that place a home. You can see, then, that at the heart of God's hospitality is his generosity with himself. The primary thing he wants to restore to us is a relationship with him, because it is that relationship that makes us at home in the universe.

The kind of generosity then, which is manifested in the hospitality of God is both a generosity of giving, but also, and more essentially, of sharing. Jesus shows this so arrestingly when he said "And surely I am with you always, to the very end of the age." (Matthew 28:20) Jesus is generous not only with his blessings, but more importantly, with his own presence. In fact, Jesus shares himself with us so completely and intimately that he promised not only to be with us, but actually *in* us.

> [20] On that day you will realize that I am in my Father, and you are in me, and I am in you. (John 14:20)

> [27] to whom God willed to make known what is the riches of the glory of this mystery among the Gentiles, which is Christ in you, the hope of glory. (Colossians 1:27 - NASB)

> [4] "Live in me. Make your home in me just as I do in you." (John 15:4 - MSG)

So you can see that Jesus is all about sharing himself. His generous heart of hospitality is declared and explained wonderfully in John 14. We've already looked at it, but I can't help myself; we'll look at it again because it so fully illustrates my point.

> [2] "In My Father's house are many dwelling

places; if it were not so, I would have told you; for I go to prepare a place for you.
[3] "If I go and prepare a place for you, I will come again and receive you to Myself, that where I am, *there* you may be also. (John 14:2-3) (NASB)

So this passage shows us that God, in his extravagant hospitality, is not an absent Father who gives but doesn't share. He's not a stingy host who's always thinking about what it cost. Instead, through Jesus, God provides for us not just a house to live in forever, but more to the point, a house to live in *with him*. God's desire and purpose behind giving us a house is that each of us would have a special place where he can share himself intimately with us.

All of this helps us understand what it means for us to be hospitable. Genuine hospitality is not just opening my home and providing a meal, but at its heart it is the sharing of myself with another. But in order to help you get an even clearer grasp of this vital part of hospitality, let me take you one step further in the journey of generosity.

GENEROSITY STRETCHED

My first year after I graduated from college was spent in Tempe Arizona. I had moved there from California to be a youth pastor intern in a very large church. Since I had lived with my parents through college, I had never been away from home before. So at age 21 this was a very new, stretching, and lonely experience for me, and the sense of loneliness became greater as the Christmas season approached. I had always spent Christmas with family, and loved all the traditions that were part of the way we celebrated the Season. Now here I was in a strange place with no one familiar around me. I found myself feeling rather depressed as people at church talked about what their families did for Christmas – the joyful celebrations and gatherings that comprised their observance of the birthday of Jesus – knowing that I was alone and couldn't go home for Christmas because of my responsibilities at church. Even though there were some two thousand people in the church, no one had invited me to be included with them, nor did I expect them to. I had never experienced including strangers in my Christmas celebrations at home, so it didn't even cross my mind that anyone would include me. It was kind of outside my frame of reference.

Well, you can imagine my surprise, and my joy, when just a few days before Christmas a family asked me if I would like to celebrate the Holiday with them in their mountain cabin. Mike and Jewel, along with their two teenage sons and one daughter were like a warm blanket on a very chilly evening to me that

Christmas. They were appalled when they found out I had not been invited to participate in anyone's plans, and quickly made provision to include me as part of their celebration. I remember weeping with relief and gratitude that I wouldn't have to spend Christmas alone. The "cabin" was a beautiful house in Pine Top Arizona, with a huge stone fireplace, a roaring fire, snow outside (I had never been in the snow on Christmas, and it was awesome!), and we had the best possible time together. I was made to feel part of things – welcome and included. It was as if Jesus himself had put his arms around me, and I saw it as the fulfillment of his promise in Luke 18:

> [29] "I tell you the truth," Jesus said to them, "no one who has left home or wife or brothers or parents or children for the sake of the kingdom of God
> [30] will fail to receive many times as much in this age and, in the age to come, eternal life."
> (Luke 18:29-30)

So, with that in mind, think with me for a moment about special holidays. There's Thanksgiving and Christmas, of course. And there is also Easter, the Fourth of July, and Valentine's Day, along with special holidays unique to certain locales. For instance Charleston has the Spoleto Festival, New Orleans has Mardi Gras, Santa Barbara has Fiesta, and Seattle has Seafair. All of these special occasions are usually times of tradition when we gather with family to celebrate. But it has been my observation over most of my life that families tend to jealously guard these times as distinctive "family-only" gatherings. I know there are many wonderful exceptions like the story I just related, but in my experience it is generally the case that these special occasions are closed to outsiders. But, I'd ask you to have an open mind and consider with me, for a moment, another perspective.

Most of us know at least a few people that I call "orphans." And by orphans I mean individuals or families that, like me that year in Arizona, have no other relatives around to celebrate these particular occasions with. They could be college students away from home, or single men and women whose families live far away, or people serving in the military, or nuclear families with no extended family nearby. This is a group of people desperately in need of the generous hospitality of other families or individuals around them. The sense of homelessness for orphans during these times is particularly acute. They need to be included in holiday celebrations, but this can only happen if we open our hearts, homes, and family traditions in a spirit of generosity and include them in our times together, like Mike and Jewel did for me.

Since we have been married my wife and I have made it a practice to include these dear folks in our family celebrations whenever possible. We always have an eye open for people at church or in other venues who might fit into my orphan category, and invite them to celebrate with us at Christmas or Easter or other holidays. Opening your family traditions to share hospitably with other people may be a stretch for you, but I'd urge you to consider my story, and ask God to open your heart to this kind of generosity. If you do, you may very well be the loving arms of Jesus around a lonely and hurting soul.

INVITED HOME

VI. ENTERTAINING ANGELS

We can see clearly that God is a loving God who has entered the lives of men and women to help them find a way back home. And we can see that hospitality is the very practical way in which God manifests that love. But the wonderful thing is that in that same spirit of hospitality, God is inviting us, even urging us to join him, sharing in his mission to transform and heal the last, least, and lost; the lonely and outcast and forsaken…people just like you and me.

Put simply, God commands his people to practice hospitality. "Share with God's people who are in need. Practice hospitality." (Romans.12.13) So, my purpose in this chapter on God's mandate regarding hospitality, is to show you that it is not just some optional thing for us to do if we happen to have the time, or if it's something we enjoy, or if we have the gift of hospitality. It's not something we can keep on the back burner to think about later if, and when, our lives become less busy. It's not something to be left to those who have nice houses, and pretty dining rooms, and who know how to cook and put on a lovely dinner. Rather, as we've seen, hospitality is something central to the very character of God, and as such is necessary to be demonstrated by his people if we are going to rightly represent him to the watching world. If we want people to really see what God is like, hospitality should ooze from every pore - it should dominate our lives and be one of the primary activities in which we engage. Imagine a world in which every Christian individual, and every Christian household, and organization, and church and community blazingly radiated the hospitality of God. Think of the people whose lives would be transformed; the psychologists offices with a shortage patients; the jails with a scarcity of prisoners; the streets with a paucity of homeless; the bars with a dearth drunks; living rooms emptied of their sad and lonely TV-watching souls, all because God's people took seriously his call to practice hospitality.

But I also want to communicate this important calling from God in a manner that isn't weighty with ought-ness and duty and obligation, because I don't believe that is the spirit in which it is communicated in the Bible. It is my heart's desire for each of you to see that hospitality is a delightful, exciting, joyful, adventuresome way to serve God, and that it accomplishes some of the most serious, weighty and wonderful things in the lives of the people it touches. Hospitality is an important, powerful, significant adventure that God commands us to engage in.

With that in mind, I think it's helpful to see that God urges us toward hospitality in not only one of my favorite verses in the Bible, but also one of the most intriguing:

> "Don't forget to show hospitality to strangers, for some who have done this have entertained angels without knowing it!" (Heb.13.2)(NLT)

Now this verse really gets me going! I've always had a thing about angels. I'm completely fascinated by accounts of them in the Bible. Angels are an entirely different race of beings; powerful, glorious, un-fallen, with the ability to travel between this world and heaven, and perhaps be in both places at the same time. Because they are without sin, their view of reality is not clouded or confused like ours, so they are able to worship and love God entirely and without any reservation. And since they are able to serve him without the limitations of our human weaknesses, they do so with unspeakable skill, unshakeable resolve, unfathomable knowledge, unalloyed purity of purpose, and unimaginable power. No wonder they are so awesome that their very presence usually causes a human being to cower in fear like the shepherds that first Christmas day;

> And there were shepherds in the same country abiding in the field, and keeping watch by night over their flock. And an angel of the Lord stood by them, and the glory of the Lord shone round about them: and they were sore afraid. (Luke 2:8-9) (ASV)

Sometimes an angel would even cause a person to fall down in a dead faint, like Daniel in his encounter with the angel Gabriel;

> As I, Daniel, was trying to understand the meaning of this vision, someone who looked like a man stood in front of me. And I heard a voice calling out from the Ulai River, "Gabriel, tell this man the meaning of his vision." As Gabriel approached the place where I was standing, I became so terrified I fell with my face to the ground. But Gabriel roused me with a touch and helped me to my feet. (Daniel 8.15-17a) (NLT)

And speaking of Gabriel, we meet him again in the

New Testament with a very important announcement. He appeared to a priest named Zechariah to tell him that in his old age he would become a father, and his son would be great, and would have a unique place in God's salvation history, preparing God's people for the coming of the Messiah. By his response, you can see how deeply wounded Zechariah was because of the decades of his wife Elizabeth's barrenness. How long had they both prayed that God would give them a child, and how many years had passed with no answer? So even the unnerving appearance of the angel Gabriel, one of the most shockingly powerful and overwhelmingly glorious beings ever created by God, was not enough to free him from his skepticism;

> Zechariah said to the angel, "How can I be sure this will happen? I am an old man now, and my wife is also well along in years." (Luke 1.18) (NLT)

I love Gabriel's response;

> Then the angel said "I am Gabriel! I stand in the very presence of God. It was He who sent me to bring you this good news..." (Luke 1.19) (NLT)

It's like Gabriel was saying "Do you have ANY idea who I am, and where I come from?" And I can imagine that with each word Gabriel became larger, and brighter, and more terrifying. And it would be forgivable to speculate that once those words came from Gabriel's mouth, Zechariah fell to his knees and wept with joy at the knowledge that God had finally answered his prayer, and had even sent someone as awesome as the angel Gabriel to give him the news.

Can you see why I'm fascinated by angels? They are astonishing beings that most of us have never seen, but who participate significantly in the affairs of men at God's bidding. In (Hebrews 1.14) we are told that angels are "…ministering spirits sent out to serve those who are going to inherit salvation…" Further, ever since reading The Space Trilogy by C. S. Lewis, my imagination has been even more active about this subject, and I've very much wanted to have an encounter with an angel.

"I was just preparing to rise again and hunt systematically round the room for a candle when I heard Ransom's name pronounced; and almost, but not quite, simultaneously I saw the thing I had feared so long to see. I heard Ransom's name pronounced: but I should not like to say I heard a voice pronounce it. The sound was quite astonishingly unlike a voice. It was perfectly articulate: it was even, I suppose, rather beautiful...The two syllables sounded more as if they were played on an instrument than as if they were spoken: and yet they did not sound mechanical either...this was more as if rock or crystal or light had spoken of itself. And it went through me from chest to groin like the thrill that goes through you when you think you have lost your hold while climbing a cliff." (Perelandra, C. S. Lewis; The McMillan Company, New York; 1965. P.17-18)

Well, I could go on and on about angels, but I must return to my point - a difficult thing indeed for a preacher to do! But I felt it was appropriate to explore just briefly the subject of angels because of the fact that there is definitely a connection between them and the joyous adventure, and serious task of hospitality. Remember the verse I pointed out at the beginning of this chapter;

> "Don't forget to show hospitality to strangers, for some who have done this have entertained angels without knowing it!" (Heb.13.2)(NLT)

So, if you're anything like me and would love, someday, to have an angelic encounter, practicing hospitality is the one thing you can do to possibly affect that outcome. Wouldn't it be cool to have dinner with an angel; to listen to what he had to say, and experience how he might instruct, or encourage, or strengthen your faith ... perhaps helping you to walk more deeply into God's purpose for your life so that you could live more effectively and meaningfully? Now, of course, there are many other ways God can accomplish those things in your life, but sometimes I'm sure he uses angels to help. So what a serious thing, and what an adventure it is to be hospitable to people, and especially to strangers, knowing that there might be angels involved.

And yet whether angels ever come into the picture or not, hospitality is still an adventure and a calling. It is in the practice of hospitality that I have experienced more human/divine help and healing than in almost any other experience. Let me tell you of a recent example.

Just a few months ago we had dear friends, Jason and Jessica, visiting us from Seattle. At our urging they came to spend about four days with us. Jason has allowed me the privilege of mentoring him since his college days, and as couples the four of us have spent many significant and enjoyable times together over delicious dinners. We wanted them to see the beautiful place we have moved to (California wine country), to have a break from the dreary Seattle gray and rain, and to have a respite from their two beautiful young children. We also wanted to simply spend some time with them because we missed them very much since they were an important part of our lives in Seattle. Though Becky and I are about 35 years their senior, there seems to be very little generation gap in our friendship. Nevertheless we thought it would be fun, during their stay with us, to have another younger couple share dinner with us. Paul and Rheanna are new friends, but already have a special place in our hearts, and we felt that the four of them would really enjoy and encourage each other. Dare I say that I felt God was urging me to facilitate this dinner? Not that I heard any kind of audible voice from heaven, but I had a strong sense that God wanted the six of us to sit down over a meal and share our lives together, and so we did.

Almost right away it was clear that Jessica and Rheanna were kindred spirits. They really enjoyed each other and had easy conversation about various subjects. Jason and Paul got along like old friends and I could tell that somehow the evening was a Divine appointment; but that intuition was about to be strikingly confirmed.

About halfway through dinner Paul asked Jason and Jessica "What is your living situation?" Now that is a rather unusual question for someone to ask complete strangers, and later Jason admitted to me that he wondered what in the world Paul was getting at. But as I heard the question my thought was "OK God, what are you up to?" I was fascinated because I, unlike Paul, knew how significant a question it was. Because of some extremely difficult circumstances in their lives, Jason and Jessica are living in her parents' basement. They are very grateful for the accommodation, but strongly desire a place of their own. Jason, like most young men, wants to provide for his family, and feels a great deal of tension because of their present circumstances. So their answer to Paul's question was cautious but honest, sharing about living in their parents' basement. Paul's response was something like this; "I know it's a strange question, but I can't get past the very strong sense that God is telling me he has a house for you guys."

Now Jason, although a strong believer and on a good path toward maturity in the faith, is fairly skeptical about "words from God" from other people about the specifics of his life. This is not necessarily a bad thing, depending on where that skepticism comes from. But in this case, as soon as Paul said "I think God is telling me he has a house for you guys," Jason and Jessica both started to cry. Jason is not the kind of guy who cries easily or openly, especially in front of strangers, but this word had such a powerful impact on him that tears simply had to flow.

I have to tell you that to me, especially with men, tears are a holy thing. When a man cries in my presence I usually feel I'm on holy ground because those tears are flowing from a very private, very vulnerable place. So as I'm watching this happen at our dinner table I'm thinking that God is doing something very significant that I'm privileged to be a part of. Because I wanted to understand more clearly what was happening, I asked Jason to tell us what he was thinking and feeling ... why did what Paul shared with him make him cry?

He explained that although he doesn't believe this theologically, emotionally he tends to be a deist. That is, to some degree he feels about life that God created the universe and then just left it alone to run by itself without much personal interest or involvement. Jason said that unfortunately this tends to make him somewhat skeptical and cynical about God. And now he is hearing a person who he doesn't know tell him that God may have given that person an insight that specifically addresses a very current and very hot issue in his own life. Jason was explaining that in some wonderful way this puts the lie to his skepticism and deism.

Can you see what a formidable - even supernatural

work was going on here? The wounds of disappointments and broken dreams can make us believe the lie that God is distant and uncaring. And that lie can steal hope and joy from our lives. But God used hospitality to bring a healing and encouraging word to a hurting couple, and to begin to dissipate a serious kind of darkness from their lives. Perhaps angels actually were involved!

Now I'm sure my friend Paul is not an angel, but in a very real sense he was sent by God as a "ministering spirit" to Jason and Jessica, and perhaps angels were helping him. But the point of all this is that it happened in the context of hospitality, ***and would not have happened otherwise.*** It was because Becky and I reached out to the four of them to have dinner in our home, and because they responded with a "yes", that this experience was able to unfold. A significant breakthrough in Jason's relationship with God was initiated around that dinner table because of hospitality. Paul was vulnerable, open, and welcoming enough (read "hospitable") to share what he thought God might be saying to him about Jason and Jessica. And Jason and Jessica were similarly open to Paul and Rheanna so they were able to hear and receive a word that God had particularly prepared for them that evening. Jason wept as he felt his skepticism and cynicism toward God being melted away. He was able to see, for a moment at least, that in spite of all the evil in this fallen world God is good and he is able and willing to help him in the specifics of life. An adventure of significance indeed!

I hope these stories are helping you see that hospitality might be a calling which would be a meaningful and worthwhile way to expend some of your time and energy and creativity; and that there is, as a result, a growing desire in your heart to respond to God's mandate to practice hospitality. But let me add a bit more fuel to the fire.

Another helpful perspective on God's call to hospitality is seen in the way he treats the subject in the Old Testament. Notice the similarities in the following three passages from the Pentateuch about why we should be hospitable to others;

> 33 ' When a stranger resides with you in your land, you shall not do him wrong. 34 ~'The stranger who resides with you shall be to you as the native among you, and you shall love him as yourself, for you were aliens in the land of Egypt; I am the Lord your God. (Lev 19:33-34) (NASB)

> 18 He executes justice for the orphan and the widow, and shows His love for the alien by giving him food and clothing. 19 So show

your love for the alien, for you were aliens in the land of Egypt. (Deut. 10:18-19) (NASB)

17 " You shall not pervert the justice due an alien *or* an orphan, nor take a widow's garment in pledge. 18 But you shall remember that you were a slave in Egypt, and that the Lord your God redeemed you from there; therefore I am commanding you to do this thing. 19 " When you reap your harvest in your field and have forgotten a sheaf in the field, you shall not go back to get it; it shall be for the alien, for the orphan, and for the widow, in order that the Lord your God may bless you in all the work of your hands. 20 When you beat your olive tree, you shall not go over the boughs again; it shall be for the alien, for the orphan, and for the widow. 21 "When you gather the grapes of your vineyard, you shall not go over it again; it shall be for the alien, for the orphan, and for the widow. 22 You shall remember that you were a slave in the land of Egypt; therefore I am commanding you to do this thing. (Deut.24:17-22) (NASB)

You can see that in all three instances God commands his people to show love by an open welcome, and by generously feeding and caring for those who are lonely and lost - strangers in a strange land. And notice that in all three examples the reason he gives for treating others in this way is because of the way God had treated them. They were slaves and aliens in Egypt, homeless and mistreated and without a place to call their own. But God, with a mighty hand and an outstretched arm, freed them from their slavery and carried them in love and mercy to a place to call their own - a home that would welcome them and generously supply their needs. And since they were the beneficiaries of God's largesse in this wonderful way, it is only right that they extend the same love and mercy to others who suffer similarly.

In the New Testament we see this same reasoning applies to God's people because of how he has freed them from their slavery to sin through Jesus.

> 10 Herein is love, not that we loved God, but that he loved us, and sent his Son *to be* the propitiation for our sins. 11 Beloved, if God so loved us, we also ought to love one another. (1 John 4:10-11) (ASV)

So, to put it simply, since God has been hospitable to us, we also ought to be hospitable to one another. And the wonderful thing is, as I stated in an earlier chapter, this call to hospitable love is not something we have to dredge up out of some kind of obligation or duty, but in fact is something that God has already put in our hearts when we believed in Jesus.

> 5 and hope does not disappoint, because the love of God has been poured out within our hearts through the Holy Spirit who was given to us. (Romans 5:5) (NASB)

If you're a Christian then, you already have the hospitable love of God in your heart. And I know that some of you are saying to yourselves "I think maybe they skipped me when they were passing that out." But I assure you they did not, and that the Apostle Paul had all of us in mind when he said what he said in Rom.5. But as with many of these things, we have to cultivate a closer relationship to Jesus in order to discover the reality of what he's put within us. So I would encourage you to meditate carefully on some of the stories of Jesus' hospitality that I've already shared with you. As you do so, think about the many ways Jesus has been hospitable to you, and your heart will begin to be filled with his love, and you'll find you can't help but want to be hospitable to others.

My pastor helpfully illustrated this idea recently. The influence of the culture around you can impact and change your life. For example, if you spend some time in Spain you find that the siesta is something embedded in the culture. While there, perhaps you start taking a siesta yourself, and find that you really enjoy the practice. So when you come back to the United States you decide you are going to continue that practice here, even though it's not something Americans are used to. By the same token, Paul is saying in (Romans 5.5) that since we believed in Jesus, the Holy Spirit (the "culture" of the Trinity) has been poured into us, and He is influencing the way we live our lives. The culture of God's hospitable love is influencing and replacing the culture of selfishness and self-absorption that is native to our character.

But here's the thing; some of us Christians have no sense of that cultural influence on us. We may have genuine faith in God…a real relationship with Jesus…but have no desire to open our hearts and homes to others, no hospitable stirrings within. Many Christians are crabbed and prickly and curmudgeonly, and walk around with expressions on their faces as if they were pickled in formaldehyde. (Come on, you know who you are!) Does that mean Paul was wrong when he said that the love of God has been poured out in our hearts through the Holy Spirit? Not at all. It simply means you have been spending too much time in America, and not enough time in Spain. Spiritual growth and spiritual health are only accomplished by foreign travel. We need an experience of cultural immersion in order to discover existentially what God has revealed to be true about us. We need to spend plenty of time in Spain practicing the custom of siesta until it gets into our blood. Then, when we come back to the US, we need to continue that practice. If we do it faithfully and with enough grace, then others might even take up the same habit themselves, and this cultural influence will spread, and many people will be influenced for good.

The wonderful thing about it is that we can all travel to Spain any time we want, without the hassle of having to spend a lot of money on airplane tickets, making sure our passports are up to date, packing suitcases, and braving transatlantic flights in seats designed by the Marquis de Sade.

The Holy Spirit is ready and eager to immerse us in the culture of the Trinity whenever we turn to God in prayer, or spend time meditating on his word, or adoring him in praise and worship, or reading some good book that helps us believe more authentically, or having a conversation with a friend that brings glory to God. *This* is spiritual Spain-travel. In fact, the more you engage in foreign travel, the less it seems foreign, and over time you may discover that your citizenship has actually been changed – that as C.S. Lewis put it, your true home is in Aslan's country. And your job is to bring the influence of that country back to what *was* your home, in order to help others find their way to their true home as well.

So, we have seen that the culture of the Trinity is essentially hospitable. God is a hospitable God, and when we are immersed in him, we bring that hospitable heart back home with us in a way that helps and heals others, and manifests to them the truth about God's welcoming heart and holy character. *That* is why God exhorts us to practice hospitality. That is the adventure we are called to.

Now I'd like to ask your indulgence as I approach this subject from one more angle. And the reason I want to take the time with you to do this is that so often we're exhorted to do what God says, but are not shown *how* to do it. Frequently we're told that the Bible says we ought to act differently, but are then left with the impression that it's up to us to work up our will power and get on with it. We're prodded to conform to Biblical behavior, but left to think that the power to accomplish this behavior must come from us. But fortunately that's not the case! The Bible isn't calling us to rely on human strength to accomplish super-human tasks. God is not asking us to be humanistic in the way we live our lives, pulling ourselves up by our own boot-straps. "God helps those who help themselves" is a popular phrase, but it is not in the Bible, and it isn't the way God designed us to live our lives.

So what do I do about it? It is one thing to see that I need to be generous, and to move beyond giving to sharing, and that selfishness and greed produce death; and it is quite another thing to actually have a heart full of generosity. What if I suffer from Nabal's stony-heart syndrome? I see that God exhorts us to practice hospitality, and invites us on this great adventure. Perhaps I'm really a believer, and want to follow him in this calling. But what if I still feel empty inside, with little or nothing to share? I see that I need a change of heart, but what am I supposed to do about that?

Remember that first and foremost, God is hospitable *to you*. He is not asking you to do your best to offer more out of your own empty life. Rather, he is inviting you to receive afresh from the generosity of the Host of Heaven. God is eager to have you dine at his table, and when you do you find plenty to eat. ("You prepare a table before me in the presence of my enemies; you anoint my head with oil; my cup overflows." Ps.23.5 HCSB). It is there that you are filled up with the assurance that you are valuable. At his table you find peace that passes understanding, new mercies every morning, grace sufficient for every need, the wide and long and high and deep love of Jesus. So take some time to indulge yourself at God's banquet. There is no need to count calories or restrict your intake at his meal – the only thing that will grow bigger and softer there is your heart.

OK, fine, but how do I do that? What do you mean, "...take some time to indulge yourself at God's banquet."? Well, we're talking here about spiritual growth, so it must relate to the intake of spiritual food. What is there in life that will nurture the spiritual part of our being? The Bible says about itself that *it* is spiritual food.

> [2] like newborn babies, long for the pure milk of the word, so that by it you may grow in respect to salvation...(1 Peter 2:2) (NASB)

> [103] How sweet are Your words to my taste! *Yes, sweeter* than honey to my mouth! (Psalm 119:103) (NASB)

> [12] "I have not departed from the command of His lips; I have treasured the words of His mouth more than my necessary food. (Job 23:12) (NASB)

> [16] Your words were found and I ate them, And Your words became for me a joy and the delight of my heart; For I have been called by

Your name, O LORD God of hosts.
(Jeremiah 15:16) (NASB)

Here then are just a few of many examples in the
Bible that tell us God's Word is food for the soul.
His Word fills us with his truth, his thoughts, his
point of view, and even his very presence.   God
makes himself present to the person who ingests his
Word with an open heart and mind.   So that is one
specific thing you can do to feast at God's table.
Gobble up his word.   It may take some patience, but
over time you will find things are taking place inside
of you.   You are growing stronger, and more full of
God's grace.

An additional, practical way to feast at God's table is
to practice God's presence.   (See "The Practice of
the Presence of God" by Brother Lawrence.)   What
this means, briefly, is to simply, by faith, affirm that
God is present with you, to you, and in you.   It can
include meditation and prayer, but can also be an
attitude of prayer throughout the day as you go
about the mundane things of life.   But these are
various ways to "abide" in Jesus; to feast on his
person and presence and experience intimacy with
him.   Here are some places in the Bible that suggest
this experience;

[4] "Abide in Me, and I in you. As the branch

cannot bear fruit of itself unless it abides in the vine, so neither *can* you unless you abide in Me.

[5] "I am the vine, you are the branches; he who abides in Me and I in him, he bears much fruit, for apart from Me you can do nothing.(John 15:4-5) (NASB)

[35] Jesus said to them, "I am the bread of life; he who comes to Me will not hunger, and he who believes in Me will never thirst. (John 6:35) (NASB)

[48] I am the bread of life.
[49] Your fathers ate the manna in the wilderness, and they died.
[50] This is the bread that comes down from heaven so that anyone may eat of it and not die. (John 6:48-50) (HCSB)

[20] Teach these new disciples to obey all the commands I have given you. And be sure of this: I am with you always, even to the end of the age." (Matthew 28:20) (NLT)

So here we see that Jesus invites us to practice his presence. ("Abide" in him.) He tells us that he himself is food for our soul, so practicing his presence will nourish us in the ways we need. And he promises that we never have to beg him for these gifts of nourishment...that we can count on him to be **with us always**, so we simply need to receive his presence by faith – to believe he is present with us because he promises he will be, and we know that God cannot lie, and his word cannot be broken.

My point is that true hospitality – embracing other people in love and welcome – is the overflow of God's cultural influence in our lives. It is what is manifested through us as we are filled up at his banquet. It is not from love born of lack – a kind of need or emptiness that we are to practice hospitality. And it is not out of the attempt to gain points with God that true hospitality emerges from our lives. That would be the practice of religion rather than hospitality. But as we've seen from the example of the Pharisees, religion can never be hospitable. Rather, as we feed at God's table, hospitality is the gurgling up of what the Bible calls "rivers of living water" that flow out of us and into others and bring them life, encouragement, comfort, the sense of finding their way back home again.

Can you see how learning to be hospitable doesn't just start with learning some new recipe, or buying a new set of dinner dishes? It starts with the preparation of your own heart, bringing it into harmony with the heart of God. But let me quickly add that this doesn't mean you have to wait until you've reached some vague and unquantifiable level of spiritual maturity. It simply means that we all need to be in the process of spiritual growth in order for our expression of hospitality to become richer and more genuine. And often spiritual growth involves simply the obedience of doing. This is not meant to contradict in any way what I've just said in the last several pages. However the truth is, sometimes we simply need to step out in faith and obey God's call to hospitality before we experience his love flowing through us. Sometimes God doesn't give you what you need until you step out and do. For example, in Joshua 3&4 God told the nation of Israel that he was going to stop the Jordan River from flowing so that they could cross into the Promised Land on dry ground. The river was at flood stage so they couldn't have crossed it otherwise. But there was a condition; God said to Joshua "Tell the priests who carry the Ark of the Covenant: When you reach the edge of the Jordan's waters, go and stand in the river." (Josh.3.8) It wasn't until they got their feet wet that the waters of the Jordan actually stopped flowing. Sometimes we have to step out and get our feet wet before we can really walk into the Promised Land of the fullness of God's ministry through us. So if you're one of those who experiences fear, or dread, or burden when you consider the idea of being hospitable, let me encourage you, along with feasting at God's table, to take little steps of obedience toward this important calling. Get your feet wet! If you do, you're liable to discover a wonderful journey that God has been patiently waiting to include you in. And you might even find yourself feeling badly that you waited so long, because you're having such a great time engaging in such an important task.

VII. SOMETHING VALUABLE TO SHARE

So far we have seen not only that God is full of generous hospitality, but also that he urges us to soak up his hospitality like a sponge so that it becomes part of us and we live out those same loving, hospitable impulses toward others. I have to have a heart that is prepared to both give and receive hospitality before I can actually *be* hospitable.

But I have found that there is one other significant roadblock to hospitality that must be overcome by many people in order for this wonderful ministry to come to fruition in our lives. In order for me to open my heart and home to people and invite them to share life with me, I must have the certainty that I have something valuable to share with them. And ultimately what I need to be certain of is that the valuable thing I have to share with others is…are you ready…ME MYSELF.

"Now wait a minute!" I can hear you say. "Isn't that a little arrogant? I mean, I thought humility was one of the primary character qualities that God wants me to have. This sounds like just the opposite. How can I see myself as the primary thing of value I have to share with others and still be humble?"

I know, I know. It seems counter-intuitive doesn't it? But I believe after you hear my explanation you will see what I'm getting at, and see the truth that, rightly held, it is the most humble possible approach to life. And I think an experience I just recently had will help to clarify this idea.

Some months ago my 45th high school reunion took place. As is often the case in these situations, because so much time had gone by no one in charge was able to find out how to contact me, so I didn't hear about the reunion and therefore didn't attend. Subsequently Bruce, an old high school friend, curious about what had happened to me, was able to get in touch. "Where the heck have you been, and why weren't you at the reunion?" he crackled at me over the phone. "Everybody was pinging me about you – where's Mike Dietrich, where's Mike Dietrich!? Next time you're in Santa Barbara, you've got to call Jeff and Dottie – they've been trying to get in touch with you for several years."

Santa Barbara is where I grew up and went to high school and college. And Jeff and Dottie are old high school friends – some of the dearest people I know. They married after high school, and we have had infrequent but fond contact over the 45 years since. Becky and I used to travel to Santa Barbara every few years to visit my mom, but since she died we have had less reason to go there. Yet we still manage to visit from time to time, and whenever we do I always think about contacting Jeff and Dottie. But here's my problem; my view of Jeff and Dottie has always been that they out-class me by a mile, so I never contacted them because I felt I would just be an imposition on them, and "...why would they be interested in interacting with me anyway?" They never gave me reason to feel this way. They were always sweet, affirming, kind and loving. The issue, of course, is me. It is all about my view of myself. It is the idea that in my own mind I have little or nothing of value to share with other people – that no one would value contact with me. And the result of this kind of view of myself is the creation of the fear of rejection. It's the idea that since I don't think I have much value, I believe somewhere in the depths of my heart, and sometimes unawares, that any attempt at opening my life to someone and reaching out to them hospitably would be met with a polite "No thank you." Since that polite "No thank you" would only serve to confirm my sense of worthlessness, I simply play it safe and avoid reaching out to people at all.

That is why, for years I never contacted Jeff and Dottie. It was self-protection produced by my low sense of worth. But in this case, spurred on by the knowledge that they had been trying to get in touch with me, I did make contact, we ended up having dinner together, and it was one of the most delightful, joyful reunions between old friends that I can remember. We rehearsed old memories, shared about life's triumphs and tragedies, laughed and cried, talked about hope for the future, and prayed together for God's help and encouragement in this next phase of our lives.

Now I realize that this experience is not a rare or unusual response to life for many people. Some of you reading this can identify very closely with what I've described. In fact I may even have succeeded in uncovering old wounds that you had almost forgotten about – perhaps because you have experienced genuine rejection in your life. Maybe you've had special friendships that have gone sour – people with whom you were once close but who, for whatever reason, no longer desire to be in relationship with you. Maybe you've suffered through a divorce, or a church split, or dysfunctional parenting, or some other relational trauma. But whatever the experience, life can come in on us in very damaging ways, and make us retreat from relationships, and retreat from hospitality.

"OK good," you might be thinking. "He understands this, and so does God, so I'm the exception to the rule. I can just relax, and I needn't bother myself further about the whole hospitality thing. I can simply continue to live in self-protection mode and limit myself to the small circle of very safe friendships already established in my life."

Au contraire, mon ami! I hate to pop your bubble, but since we've seen that hospitality is an important part of the heart of God, and since hospitality is therefore a significant part of God's calling to all of us who believe in Him, it is simply not an option to remain disengaged from this ministry of welcome to others. Because God loves you and me, and because in that love he desires the best for us, including the growth and expansion of our lives for his glory, there are no special exemptions. And yet I just told you a story of my own struggle with hospitality because of the fear of rejection and the instinct for self-protection. How can I move beyond that fear? Do I just grit my teeth, get over myself, screw up my self-effort, and push forward? After all, not everyone will have a friend like Bruce who calls and assures them that so-and-so really wants to see them. What's the answer?

Well fortunately, there is an answer, and it's a wonderful one. It is *not* that we simply have to try harder for God. It is *not* a matter of gritting my teeth and getting over myself. Instead, and in sharp contrast, it is a matter of trust. It is a matter of leaning back and resting in the truth that *you yourself* are the infinitely valuable gift you bring to others because of Jesus Christ. And it's those last four words that make all the difference. It is not that you have value autonomously. It is not that you appeared in the universe because of the convergence of the impersonal, plus time, plus chance, and I am asking you to take a blind leap of faith and simply believe that you have value for no other reason than that I say so. Instead, you yourself have infinite value, and you yourself are the primary gift you bring to others, BECAUSE OF JESUS CHRIST. That is, through Jesus you are God's special creation, made in his very image. (Genesis 1.26-27; Colossians 1.15-16) Further, God demonstrates how much he values you by the way he expresses his love for you. Here are just a few examples of this truth recorded in Scripture:

[17] The LORD your God is with you, he is

mighty to save. He will take great delight in you, he will quiet you with his love, he will rejoice over you with singing." (Zephaniah 3:17)

Can you imagine this? Have you ever heard that God *sings* over you? But there it is, right there in the Bible! He delights in you so much that he actually rejoices over you with singing. And this is not because of anything you have done or not done. It is not because you have been good or bad enough to earn God's love or wrath. It is because, IN JESUS, God's freely-given love is unearned, undeserved, and unconditional. As long as you are IN JESUS, you are wrapped in God's gracious and unearned love and forgiveness. And you are in Jesus if you have believed in him...if you have lifted up the empty hands of faith and received the gift he offers to everyone. (More on that in the last chapter!) But these next four passages from the Bible are further declarations from God about how much he values you.

¹⁶ "For God so loved the world that he gave his one and only Son, that whoever believes in him shall not perish but have eternal life. ¹⁷ For God did not send his Son into the world to condemn the world, but to save the world through him. (John 3:16-17)

[8] But God proves His own love for us in that while we were still sinners, Christ died for us! (Romans 5:8) (HCSB)

[19...] You are not your own;
[20] you were bought at a price. (1 Corinthians 6:19b-20a)

[18] For you know that you were redeemed from your empty way of life inherited from the fathers, not with perishable things like silver or gold,
[19] but with the precious blood of Christ, like that of a lamb without defect or blemish. (1 Peter 1:18-19) (HCSB)

Can you see that God loves you so much that he paid an infinite price to save you? Can you see that Jesus is infinitely valuable, and that God was willing to pay the price of his life in order to redeem you (buy you back) from the penalty of sin? So let's think this through. One of the main ways we understand the value of something is to know its price. The price of a diamond versus the price of a cubic zirconia helps us see the difference in value between those two things. And what God did was to take the most valuable thing in the universe – the life of his very own Son – and spend that currency on you and me. That's how much God values us. We are bought with an infinite price; the precious blood (life) of Jesus. Therefore, we must be of infinite value in God's opinion, and since it is God's opinion that establishes ultimate reality, I can be certain that my worth rests on a rock-solid foundation, and is not just some vague hope, or the power of positive thinking, or a blind leap of faith. Are you with me? If not, read this paragraph again, because it is of titanic importance. It is the answer to all your insecurities, all your fears, all the forces that manipulate you in life, all the things that keep you narrowed and incomplete and from being fully the person that God designed you to be.

It's like the difference between having your life anchored to a foundation of jello, or to a foundation of solid granite. Your sense of worth is foundational to your very being, because without a sense of worth your life is absurd. If a person has no value, he has no purpose or reason to exist. So if someone's worth is threatened, his very life is threatened. Consequently, the material from which that worth-foundation is made, will substantially determine the stability of your life. For instance, when you derive your sense of worth from the opinions of other people, your foundation is always at risk; it's jello. This is because the opinions of others about you are always subject to the most supercilious things; the current fashion, how you smell (why, otherwise, do people spend so much on perfumes and colognes?), your tone of voice, a momentary lapse in manners, a five pound weight gain, and acne break-out...you name it. So, if you are dependent on the opinions of other people to feel worthwhile, then your sense of well-being will always be prey to the most unpredictable, capricious, uncontrollable and silly things. You are living on a foundation of jello! But if, on the other hand, you derive your sense of worth from God's opinion of you, then your foundation is granite; immovable, unchangeable, reliable, sure...because God has revealed in the Bible, as we just saw, that his opinion about you has been completely and eternally settled through Jesus. And with such a granite foundation, your worth is unshakably anchored and thus your stability in life and your sense of well-being is stronger, healthier, less vulnerable.

Have I strayed far from the subject of hospitality in addressing this issue? I don't think so, because so much of our motivation and courage to reach out to others in love and welcome depends very heavily on how we feel about our own value. If I believe I have something valuable to share, and come to understand that I myself am that thing, then I've always got something to give, and am therefore willing – and even eager – to practice hospitality. So let me encourage you to believe what God says about your worth as a person. He loves you, and sings over you. What an awesome truth!

Now that we've established a rock solid foundation for personal worth, let me be quick to affirm that I'm not saying it's an easy transition from jello to granite. Remember the story I told you about Jeff and Dottie – my friends from high school? Obviously that was a clear example of someone (me) who still has jello under his feet. The truth of the matter is that many of us vacillate back and forth from jello to granite due to a number of factors. In my case, when I see myself reacting to life out of a sense of worthlessness, I am usually able to affirm the truth, lean back on Jesus, and step out in faith. It's not always easy for me, but over the years I've found that when I rest in God's truth about these issues, I'm usually able to emerge from my fears and engage with people in welcoming love. In fact most people who know me will tell you they don't really believe I'm fearful in the way I've described. The reason for that is I've become fairly good at quickly transitioning from fear to rest by reviewing in my heart and mind what the Bible reveals as God's opinion about me. So I can assure you that what I'm talking about here comes from years of experience, and is not just a lot of theoretical mumbo-jumbo.

It's my strong desire to give you some practical help if you are one of those people who struggle with their sense of worth. So I hope you will consider these things, and that they will help encourage you in reaching out hospitably to others. After all, you have the most valuable thing possible to share with them – YOU!

But before we quit this chapter, I have one other component of this very important subject to share with you. It has to do with your unique giftedness. Up to this point we have focused on God's opinion of you. But in addition I want you to consider with me the idea that part of your value is wrapped up in the unique way God has put you together as a person.

THE VALUE OF YOUR UNIQUENESS

Not only has God created each one of us with intrinsic value because we are made in his image; and not only has he further demonstrated our value by spending an infinite price on us to redeem us from sin and its consequences; but he has also created each one of us uniquely. According to people who know about such things, no two snowflakes are exactly alike. (I always wondered how they figured that out!) Can you imagine that out of the trillions and gazillions of snowflakes that have ever fallen, not one ever looked exactly like another? God, in his infinite creativity and variety, by the same token, makes no two people exactly alike. Even identical twins are really quite different. I have identical twin granddaughters – Alyssa and Alexis – and when they were first born I couldn't tell them apart at all. But as I got to know them I began to see that they were very different not only in their looks, but in their personalities and their perspectives. They are both merciless manipulators, but one does it with a pouty lower lip and a sad look, while the other does it with a dazzling smile and a kiss. Both tactics seem to work, especially when accompanied by "I love you grandpa!" But I digress.

My point is that God has created each of us uniquely, and he has done so for a purpose. The Bible talks about how God has given each person particular gifts. These gifts are of myriad kinds and combinations. Some of God's gifts are given in the form of talents, abilities and personalities, as well as all the unique physical traits possessed by each person. Further, among those who are believers, God gives another category of gifts called "spiritual gifts." And the wonderful thing is that God has created us in this very complicated diversity so we can each contribute uniquely to one another. This can be seen in many places in the Bible but one of my favorite examples, which puts it all together very explicitly, is in Ephesians.

7 However, he has given each one of us a

special gift through the generosity of Christ.

[8] That is why the Scriptures say, "When he ascended to the heights, he led a crowd of captives and gave gifts to his people."...

[11] Now these are the gifts Christ gave to the church: the apostles, the prophets, the evangelists, and the pastors and teachers.

[12] Their responsibility is to equip God's people to do his work and build up the church, the body of Christ.

[13] This will continue until we all come to such unity in our faith and knowledge of God's Son that we will be mature in the Lord, measuring up to the full and complete standard of Christ.

[14] Then we will no longer be immature like children. We won't be tossed and blown about by every wind of new teaching. We will not be influenced when people try to trick us with lies so clever they sound like the truth.

[15] Instead, we will speak the truth in love, growing in every way more and more like Christ, who is the head of his body, the church.

[16] ***He makes the whole body fit together perfectly. As each part does its own special work, it helps the other parts grow, so that the whole body is healthy and growing and full of love.*** (Ephesians 4:7-16

SEL) (NLT) (Italics mine)

This passage shows that each individual and uniquely gifted person has his or her own special contribution to make, and without that particular contribution, the whole community is immeasurably impoverished.

Have you ever looked at someone else and wished you were more like them? Have you ever envied the way another person carried himself, or was articulate, or how smart they were, or how at ease among others, and you just wished you had the gifts they had? What's important to understand is that when you think that way you are saying to God "I don't like the way you made me. You didn't do a very good job, or you didn't do it right, or you didn't do it the way I would have, and you made a bad call." Now most of us probably wouldn't knowingly say that out loud to God, or even quietly for that matter. But when we think in this manner, that's really what we're saying. It's a kind of self-loathing insecurity that springs from a rejection of God's loving, sovereign plan and purpose for the way he made you.

Part of the remedy for that point of view is simply to understand what Ephesians 4 is saying; that God made you the way he did because he has a unique calling for you; a special thing that only you, with your gifts and personality and distinctive make up can accomplish; an inimitable contribution that only you can make. Embracing the way God designed you will help fulfill the destiny he has created for you; it will help you accomplish the important job he has designed for you to undertake for your good, the good of others, and his glory. What could be better than that!?

So I'm encouraging you to value the way God made you, because you, *as he made you*, are the primary gift you bring to others. When you try to be somebody else rather than fully yourself in Christ, you are robbing others of the gift God made you to be to them, and of the role that only you can play in their lives. You are God's gift to the world, and held in the way I've described, focusing not on self but on God, it is not an arrogant perspective but a very humble one.

Again, what has this to do with hospitality? Well, hospitality begins with being hospitable to yourself! It is being welcoming toward the person God made you to be, and embracing the unique way he gifted you. It is allowing God's hospitality to flood your own heart, believing deep down that he values you and welcomes you warmly. *Then*, you can be hospitable to others, and share his wonderful welcome with those people he brings into your life.

VIII. GIVE AND TAKE

There is a parable in the New Testament that speaks very strongly to the issue of hospitality, but from a different perspective than what we have considered so far. It is the parable of the great banquet, found in Luke.

> Jesus replied: "A certain man was preparing a great banquet and invited many guests. At the time of the banquet he sent his servant to tell those who had been invited, 'Come, for everything is now ready.' But they all alike began to make excuses. The first said, 'I have just bought a field, and I must go and see it. Please excuse me.' Another said, 'I have just bought five yoke of oxen, and I'm on my way to try them out. Please excuse me.' Still another said, 'I just got married, so I can't

come.' The servant came back and reported this to his master. Then the owner of the house became angry and ordered his servant, 'Go out quickly into the streets and alleys of the town and bring in the poor, the crippled, the blind and the lame.' 'Sir,' the servant said, 'what you ordered has been done, but there is still room.' Then the master told his servant, 'Go out to the roads and country lanes and make them come in, so that my house will be full. I tell you, not one of those men who were invited will get a taste of my banquet." (Luke 14.16-24)

The primary point of this parable is to illustrate something about the nature of the Kingdom of God. It is showing that God's Kingdom has, at its very heart, the expression of hospitality. However the emphasis in this parable is not so much on the initiation of hospitality, but rather on how people respond to God's hospitable initiative.

In this story the invited guests all respond with some kind of excuse in their refusal of God's hospitality. One is a busy real estate investor who has important business to attend to and regretfully cannot appear. Another is excited about his new 5 ox-power car and has to take it out for a test drive. And still another has family commitments - "after all, family is my first priority" - and he sends his excuses as well. There are many things in life that keep us busy, occupied, and unavailable. And these things are often valid and important commitments. But one insight from this parable is that no amount of busy-ness is a valid excuse for being an inhospitable guest. The parable shows that to refuse an invitation is just as inhospitable as to never offer one. And although the primary point of the parable is about our inhospitable refusal of God's hospitality, it also speaks strongly to the way we respond to the hospitality of people around us – the give and take that makes hospitality possible – which is the emphasis of this chapter.

You may not have considered this before, but hospitality is not just a one-way street. It does not begin and end with the inviter - the one who opens his home or heart to another. The invited one - the guest - is just as much a player in the give and take of hospitality. In Biblical times, to refuse an offer of hospitality was seen as an insult that only an enemy would inflict. In the same way that the host was gracious, so the guest also was called to be gracious. And these implications, though often lost in our self-centered and busy culture, still hold true. Whether an invitation to break bread is accepted or rejected is fraught with relational implications. Accepting an invitation to eat with someone speaks to trust and acceptance. It says something about whether I value you or not. I may be a very busy person with a lot on my plate, but accepting the invitation of another says that I don't view myself as "above" you. It says that I see us as equal in our value, our humanity, and our need for relationship or community.

At a time in our lives when my wife and I had moved to a new town, it was very important for us to find a new church to become a part of. We settled on one that appealed to us because the pastor was a gifted and sensitive preacher, the worship was beautiful, thoughtful, and maturely led, and the people seemed friendly and out-going. It was a fairly large church - six or seven hundred people - so we knew it might take some time for us to fit in and develop close and intimate friendships. A year later we were still looking for someone who might want to include themselves in the circle of our lives. And it is not that the people were un-friendly. Our first impression was correct. Every Sunday morning people would greet us, shake hands, smile, and ask us how we were. We never felt ignored. But we found that this friendliness never extended beyond Sunday morning. We worked hard at inviting people into our home for dinner, or out for coffee after church on Sunday, but we were always politely put off. For instance, one couple which we seemed to have good interaction with, when invited for dinner could not find a free moment for the next six months. Another couple very much appreciated our invitation and would "check our calendar to see what time we might have available." After persevering with them for several months to try to pin down a time we finally relented, not wanting to be too pushy. A year later, before moving to another city, they mentioned that they were "sorry we never were able to connect."

These were just two of many such experiences in our new church. It was obvious that the people were sincerely committed to Jesus, his word, his mission in the world, and his work in their lives. But for us at least, there was something significantly missing. It seemed to be a church full of people who did not understand the importance of the hospitable guest. In fact, the parable of the Great Banquet implies, to my mind at least, that there is in some measure a relationship between our response to God's invitation to his banquet, and our response to the invitation of others. To be a hospitable guest is to see that God himself is somehow involved when others invite you into their lives and their homes. Of course, there will legitimately be times when you have to say "no" to someone who wants to invite you to a dinner or some event, but if your life is too "scheduled" to respond to someone's hospitality for six months or a year, then I would encourage you to seriously, before God, review the things that you allow to crowd out this Kingdom calling in your life. I would consider that perhaps it is very important to do some editing of your busy life style and say "no" to some of the urgent things in order to say "yes" to some of the important things. The parable of the banquet asserts that those who refuse the invitation miss out on something very important which God wants us to experience; namely, his hospitality. But again, by implication, being too busy for each other is a significant way to refuse God's hospitality. An inhospitable guest does as much to inhibit the coming of God's Kingdom as does the inhospitable host.

THE ROLE OF COURTESY

But of course being a hospitable host or guest involves much more than just sending or receiving an invitation. As we have seen, hospitality involves being considerate and thoughtful to others, with the goal of bringing a spirit of welcome, openness, acceptance, care and love to my interaction with another; to restore the sense of at-homeness that has been lost to much of human experience since the Fall. And the point of this chapter is, simply put, that both the host and guest have an important part in the experience of hospitality. But what does that mean specifically? Are there certain guidelines that I should be aware of, and is there particular wisdom that I need to gain in order to know how to be hospitable?

The answer is emphatically *yes*.

Now many of you reading this chapter have been trained in hospitality by your parents and don't need any instruction about how to be a hospitable guest or host. And yet, there are many who have never been instructed in the graces of hospitable interaction, so I am going to take a few short paragraphs to give some basic advice. And even if you know all this stuff, it might be helpful to take a quick refresher course just to stimulate your thinking on the subject - because after all, when it comes right down to it, what we're really talking about here is how to show love to people.

At this point I'm going to take the plunge and introduce the word "manners." Yes, I know; for many of you that is an archaic and irrelevant word that carries with it visions of stuffy Victorian restraints, and elaborate and arcane social taboos. All you see are raised eyebrows, and all you hear is "tisk, tisk" at the first hint of some meaningless mannerly faux pas. "Manners have gone the way of the starched collar, and good riddance," is the thinking of many in my generation and those that follow; and in some cases, with good reason.

But let me give you another perspective.

There was a very famous interior designer named Sister Parish. She had done the decorating for many prominent East Coast people including Jackie Kennedy, and she was, by all accounts, quite a snob. But according to her biography, nearly all the people who knew her had an entirely different view of her husband. Without fail they all adored him, and invariably explained that the reason for their adoration was because he was the most mannerly person they had ever met. The surprising thing was that Mr. Parish's "mannerly-ness" was described by all as his ability to make you feel at ease, at home, cared about, wanted. Manners seen in this light are not just social artifices whose purpose is to make people feel uptight about social interaction, and under condemnation if they should use the wrong fork at dinner. Rather, a person of real manners is someone who is deeply considerate of others because he values them.

For instance, a person of manners is curious about others. He wants to know what makes another person tick; the likes and dislikes, uniquenesses, gifts, foibles, passions, hurts, joys, points of view of another. Curiosity about someone says powerfully to that person that they have great value, and is one of the most important characteristics of real hospitality.

Have you ever had a conversation with a person in which you did all the listening, and he or she did all the talking? I must confess that I have been on both ends of that conversation. There have been times when I was a very good listener, but there have been other times when I monopolized the conversation in a shameless manner. Instead of give and take, I was much more interested in what I had to say than in anything the poor victim of this interaction had to contribute. I was sorely lacking in the courtesy of give and take – the love and concern and curiosity that comprises hospitality toward another.

At dinner with friends recently, a visiting stranger was also included. He demonstrated the same inhospitable lack of manners that I have seen in myself at times. He was a charming story teller, a fascinating and funny character, and had very profound insights into what the Bible says about God, and people, and life. And yet, not once did he compliment the hosts on their delicious food and generous hospitality, or ask anyone at the table about their interests, joys, and sorrows. Nevertheless, I really enjoyed the evening, but was reminded of the importance of give and take. We see this in the way Jesus interacted with people. He was interested in what they thought, felt, and feared. He "brought them out," and in so doing demonstrated that the redemptive potential of hospitality is more fully

115

realized when both parties contribute to the process in the give and take of human interaction.

But some of the "smaller" manners also add significantly to the quality of hospitality. To hold the door for a person, to say please and thank you, to not interrupt someone in conversation, to honor the likes and dislikes of a guest, to introduce strangers and help them converse with each other, to be interested in the interests of others, to wait for everyone to be served at a meal before starting to eat - all these things say in word and deed that another person is important, valuable, loved. These are some of the courtesies that make others feel welcome and appreciated and at home. A person who has good manners finds a way to take the sting out of an awkward or embarrassing moment, because he wants to preserve the dignity of others. A courteous person delights in the uniqueness of another, and overlooks much that is broken in them, because love covers a multitude of sins. This is another way God is hospitable to you and me. For example look at the courtesy of Jesus toward the woman at the well.

> [5] So he came to a town in Samaria called Sychar, near the plot of ground Jacob had given to his son Joseph.
> [6] Jacob's well was there, and Jesus, tired as he was from the journey, sat down by the well. It

was about the sixth hour.

⁷ When a Samaritan woman came to draw water, Jesus said to her, "Will you give me a drink?"

⁸ (His disciples had gone into the town to buy food.)

⁹ The Samaritan woman said to him, "You are a Jew and I am a Samaritan woman. How can you ask me for a drink?" (For Jews do not associate with Samaritans.)

¹⁰ Jesus answered her, "If you knew the gift of God and who it is that asks you for a drink, you would have asked him and he would have given you living water."

¹¹ "Sir," the woman said, "you have nothing to draw with and the well is deep. Where can you get this living water?

¹² Are you greater than our father Jacob, who gave us the well and drank from it himself, as did also his sons and his flocks and herds?"

¹³ Jesus answered, "Everyone who drinks this water will be thirsty again,

¹⁴ but whoever drinks the water I give him will never thirst. Indeed, the water I give him will become in him a spring of water welling up to eternal life."(John 4:5-26)

Here we see Jesus doing what was simply *not* done in his culture, in order to be courteous and hospitable to a woman who came to draw water at Jacob's well. The woman herself pointed out the breaking of social conventions:

> The Samaritan woman said to him, "You are a Jew and I am a Samaritan woman. How can you ask me for a drink?" (For Jews do not associate with Samaritans.) (v.9)

First, in Jesus' world Jews did not associate with Samaritans. That in itself would constitute a great scandal as far as Jews were concerned. Second, men did not strike up conversations with unaccompanied women. Third, "holy" men did not sully their reputations by engaging with women of a "certain reputation," and whether it was obvious or not, Jesus certainly knew of her checkered past – as he does with all of us. But the loving and gracious heart of God once again manifests itself in Jesus' hospitable courtesy. All traditions and social conventions are trumped by the love of God which manifested itself in the true mannerly-ness of Jesus toward the woman at the well. He not only acknowledged her presence rather than ignoring her, but put himself in the lower position by asking her a favor, and then engaged her in significant conversation regarding the things that were important in her life. "Love covers a multitude of sins," (1Pet.4.8) not only describes Jesus' approach to people, but is some of the best instruction on manners and courtesy that you'll ever find anywhere, and is great guidance on how to be hospitable to others.

INVITED HOME

IX. HARLOTS, HUSBANDS, AND HOSPITALITY

Most people, even those not very familiar with the Bible, have heard something about Joshua and the battle of Jericho. (Joshua 6). This was the occasion where Joshua and the Israelite army marched around the city of Jericho once a day for six days, and then on the seventh day they marched around the city seven times, gave a great shout, and the walls around the city fell to the ground. What an awesome experience that must have been! But there were some other important things going on behind the scenes before this crazy event took place that were very important, and give us further insight into hospitality and its far-reaching consequences in the lives of families, sometimes for generations.

The context of Joshua and the famous battle of

121

Jericho is that the nation of Israel had just spent 40 years wandering in the desert wilderness after having been released from slavery to Pharaoh in Egypt. Moses had led the nation those 40 years and had just died, handing over the responsibility of leading the Israelite nation to Joshua. So it was now Joshua's task to lead this huge group of wandering Jews across the Jordan River and into the land that God had promised to his people… "a land flowing with milk and honey." God had told them that he would empower them to drive out the inhabitants of this land that he was giving them as their own homeland, and Jericho was the first significant city that Joshua and his people encountered after crossing the Jordan. It was at this strategic place that the children of Israel were to begin to occupy the land God had promised them.

So Joshua, being the skilled tactician and responsible leader that he had learned to be over the last 40 years, decided to send spies across the Jordan to check out the situation, and especially to look into what was happening in Jericho, a city which they obviously were going to have to deal with. And it is in this context that we meet up with a very interesting and significant person by the name of Rahab.

The Bible tells us that Rahab was a prostitute whose

house was part of the city wall. (Josh.2.1 & 15) After all, if you're going to build a walled city, why not make the wall do double duty and include houses within its very structure? So you've not only got a wall that protects the city, but you've also got housing for the people who live there. It is the same idea as a castle really – fortified walls which protected its inhabitants but also served as a dwelling. Further, it is likely that Rahab's house was near the gate to this walled city, given her occupation. Jericho was an important crossroads for trade, and traveling men coming into the city would conveniently find her lodgings nearby. The result was that she was well informed about what had been going on over the years of Israel's wanderings. She had heard the great stories of what Israel's God had done, drying up the Red Sea when they came out of Egypt, and destroying the Amorite kings Sihon and Og. (Joshua 2.10)

But what is fascinating is to see how these reports about Israel's exploits affected Rahab. As she heard the stories and thought about the implications of the events surrounding Israel's wanderings, she came to an amazing and very significant conclusion. Here's how she framed it, in her own words; "When we heard of it, [Israel's deeds] our hearts melted and everyone's courage failed because of you, for the Lord your God is God in heaven above and on the earth below." (Joshua 2.11) The awesome power of God demonstrated through the obedient actions of his people caused his reputation to be spread abroad to the watching world and to produce fear, and at least in Rahab's case, faith.

God is always at work behind the scenes in ways invisible and inscrutable to us, except sometimes by hindsight. In this case he knew the woman named Rahab, just like he knows each one of us. He knew she was a prostitute, just like he knows our sins, whether visible to others or secretly held. But those sins were not the real issue as far as God's attitude toward Rahab was concerned. The issue was whether or not Rahab had a heart that would be open to receive his welcome once she had heard the truth about him. And as we saw, by her own testimony she affirmed that she had come to believe in the God of Israel. So God, working subversively behind the scenes, over many years and through untold circumstances in the life of Rahab, had found himself an ally in Jericho, in the unlikely person of Rahab the harlot.

So in the providence of God, the spies that Joshua sent to Jericho ended up staying in Rahab's house. (Joshua 2.1) Perhaps they thought that lodging in the house of a prostitute would provide them with a certain anonymity, and allow them to complete their task; prostitutes, after all, have practice in exercising a particular kind of discretion. But just as in modern times, so in the days of Joshua, discretion among prostitutes is anything but airtight, and so word quickly leaked to the king of Jericho that two Israeli spies were seen entering the house of Rahab. (Joshua 2.2)

But remember, God had already done a work in the heart of Rahab. So when the spies came to her house, she welcomed them with open arms. Her faith in God produced in her a different kind of hospitality than was typical of her reputation and her occupation. So when the king's men came to her house and ordered her to turn the spies over to them, she had already hidden them on her roof, and lied to the authorities about what had happened. (I imagine if you're a prostitute, a lie isn't that big of a deal!) Here is the record of their exchange:

> [4] But the woman had taken the two men and hidden them. She said, "Yes, the men came to me, but I did not know where they had come from.
> [5] At dusk, when it was time to close the city gate, the men left. I don't know which way they went. Go after them quickly. You may catch up with them." (Joshua 2:4-5)

The upshot of the story is that the spies got safely

away and returned to Joshua with their report. They said to him "The Lord has surely given the whole land into our hands; all the people are melting in fear because of us." (Joshua 2.24b) But before leaving her house, Rahab asked the spies to show her and her family the same hospitality she had shown them. To this they heartily agreed, and promised that the lives of Rahab and her family would be spared when Jericho was attacked. "But Joshua spared Rahab the prostitute, with her family and all who belonged to her, because she hid the men Joshua had sent as spies to Jericho – and she lives among the Israelites to this day." (Joshua 6.25.)

So throughout these events involving Rahab, we see the power of hospitality at work, bringing redemption and healing, and lifting the life of a degraded and sad woman out of the depths and into a life of meaning and significance. First, we see the hospitality of God in which, unseen by anyone, he was at work in the heart of a prostitute to bring her to faith in him. We know this to be true not only because of her testimony, but also because of the fact that God embraced her as a key ally in his plan to provide a land of promise for his people. We further see God's hospitable embrace of Rahab in what he had to say about her in the New Testament. In (Hebrews 11.31) Rahab is held up as one of the heroes of the faith because of her hospitality toward the spies. "By faith the prostitute Rahab, because she welcomed the spies, was not killed with those who were disobedient." Further, we see she is embraced not only by God, but by his people, because the record tells us "...and she lives among the Israelites to this day."

Once again, we see how hospitality works. First God initiates in hospitality, and then the person who receives that hospitality becomes hospitable herself. Rahab's hospitality toward the spies was the result of God's hospitality toward her. But in addition to that, if we broaden our look into the Biblical accounts, we discover that hospitality can produce a legacy of blessing for generations to come. (Matthew 1.5) tells us that an Israelite named Salmon married Rahab. Rahab's faith-inspired hospitality was rewarded, first, by her life being spared and being welcomed to live among the Israelites. But in addition Salmon, a respected Israelite, embraced her as his wife and rescued her from her lifestyle. Rahab went from being a prostitute to being the honored wife of a man of standing in Israel because God's hospitality produced hospitality in her and she was rewarded by the hospitality of others.

But it doesn't stop there. A little research will reveal that there is a fascinating connection between Rahab's experience in the book of Joshua and the wonderful account of a Moabite woman named Ruth in the book of Ruth.

It all starts with a Jew named Elimelech and his wife Naomi. They lived in Bethlehem but because of a famine, moved to the land of Moab for a time. Their two sons went with them and eventually married Moabite women, Orpah and Ruth. At one point all three husbands died, leaving Naomi and her two daughters-in-law rather dependent on family to get by. So although Orpah decided to stay in Moab, Ruth and Naomi went back to Bethlehem when the famine ended to try to connect with family there. This is where we meet the hero of our story, Boaz.

> [1] Now Naomi had a relative on her husband's side named Boaz. He was a prominent man of noble character from Elimelech's family. (Ruth 2:1) (HCSB)

Boaz went out to his fields to supervise the work there, and he saw Ruth and asked about her. When he found out that she was a Moabite who had come to Israel with her Jewish mother-in-law, he quickly took steps to make sure she was treated well; that she had enough water to drink and food to eat; that she took time to rest from her work in the fields, and that none of the young men took advantage of her. Here is an excerpt that describes their hospitable interaction:

¹⁰ She bowed with her face to the ground and said to him, "Why are you so kind to notice me, although I am a foreigner?"
¹¹ Boaz answered her, "Everything you have done for your mother-in-law since your husband's death has been fully reported to me: ⌊how⌋ you left your father and mother and the land of your birth, and ⌊how⌋ you came to a people you didn't previously know.
¹² May the LORD reward you for what you have done, and may you receive a full reward from the LORD God of Israel, under whose wings you have come for refuge."
¹³ "My lord," she said, "you have been so kind to me, for you have comforted and encouraged your slave, although I am not like one of your female servants." (Ruth 2:10-13) (HCSB)

Boaz went to extraordinary lengths to show hospitality to this woman who was a stranger and an alien in their land, and to make sure she felt safe and at home. And the passage shows part of the reason that he treated Ruth this way. He honored her because of her loyalty to Naomi, but also because in doing so she was putting her faith in the God of Israel. She was not only changing her homeland and leaving her relatives behind in Moab, but in moving to Israel she was embracing the God of Israel. In fact we know from chapter 1 that this was the nature of Ruth's commitment to Naomi.

> [16] But Ruth said, [to Naomi] "Do not urge me to leave you *or* turn back from following you; for where you go, I will go, and where you lodge, I will lodge. Your people *shall be* my people, and your God, my God. (Ruth 1:16) (NASB)

But I think if we look a little deeper we'll find another very significant reason for the way Boaz treated Ruth. Was it because Ruth was a beautiful woman and Boaz was attracted to her? Or was it perhaps because this was the way one was supposed to treat distant relatives in Boaz' culture? Well, those could certainly be factors about which we could speculate. But I think there's another reason that trumps everything else, and we find it quietly hiding in a passage in the New Testament. In (Matthew 1.5) it says "Salmon was the father of Boaz by Rahab…" (NASB) Yes, you read correctly; Boaz was the son of Rahab the prostitute!

The legacy of Rahab's hospitality is seen poignantly in the story of Ruth and Boaz as we piece all the details of history together. Don't you think that Boaz was likely to have a special place in his heart for a needy foreign woman who comes to his country as a stranger, in large part because of his mother Rahab who came to Israel under similar circumstances? And don't you think that the hospitality which Rahab showed to the spies, and which Israel showed to her, was very much a part of the legacy which shaped the character of Boaz? And isn't it wonderful to see how faith, expressing itself through hospitality, can bring redemption and healing out of a sad and desperate situation? How likely is it that the offspring of a prostitute will end up becoming a man of great responsibility, kind thoughtfulness, and impeccable moral character? And yet through Rahab's experience we see that the hospitable love of the God of the Bible can transform not only an individual, but even generations of a family line.

At the end of the story we find that Boaz marries Ruth, and God blesses their union in a very special way.

> [13] So Boaz took Ruth and she became his wife. Then he went to her, and the LORD enabled her to conceive, and she gave birth to a son.
> [14] The women said to Naomi: "Praise be to the LORD, who this day has not left you without a kinsman-redeemer. May he become famous throughout Israel!
> [15] He will renew your life and sustain you in your old age. For your daughter-in-law, who loves you and who is better to you than seven

sons, has given him birth." (Ruth 4:13-15)

So here, at the end of the story of Ruth and Boaz we see that hospitality was an important factor woven into the lives of many people from disparate backgrounds and experiences, and used by God to bring healing and rescue, and even to form strong and healthy families out of broken and scattered lives; harlots, husbands, and hospitality. But there's one extra fragment in this mosaic of God's sovereign plan that fits seamlessly into place in a way that only God can accomplish

> [17] The women living there said, "Naomi has a son." And they named him Obed. He was the father of Jesse, the father of David. . (Ruth 4:17)

Wow! Rahab the harlot was the great, great grandmother of King David, and ultimately a progenitor of Jesus the Messiah. God's hospitable heart is wonderfully revealed in his willingness to include even a prostitute in the bloodline of his only begotten Son. God is not a religious snob who is only hospitable to "the right people." He is the God of the broken, the messed-up, the bewildered; of all of us ensnared by sin and foolishness. The invitation to dine at his table is open to any and all who will simply turn away from their own self-reliance, and come to him in faith.

X. THE HOSPITABLE HOUSE

Up to this point we have been thinking about hospitality as an internal reality – a matter of the *heart*. True hospitality flows from a hospitable heart, and a hospitable heart is the fruit of experiencing God's welcoming love in our lives. But in this chapter I want us to see that hospitality, if it is to mean anything at all, must be manifested in the real world through the *physical*. I read a story recently that will illustrate my point.

There were some young Africans who had been in some kind of a mission school and were now in European universities on scholarships. Each of them had, at some time or another, come into the homes of missionaries and had observed various aspects of the missionaries' lives during their boyhood. They each made a similar comment which, to me, speaks very loudly to the issue at hand. Each of them said that the thing which had turned them away from Christianity was the lack of beauty in the missionaries' homes – and they were speaking of physical beauty. It is a sobering thing to see that these young men had all observed the same thing, and that it had such a titanically significant effect on them. These bright young African men had rejected the Christian faith because of the link between missionaries and a lack of concern for beauty in their homes. Somehow the character of God, and his hospitable heart was invisible to these lads because the homes of God's representatives lacked any attention to the physical aspects of hospitality.

It's not that the missionaries hadn't spent enough money on their homes, or that they needed to do some extravagant thing to impress their African neighbors. Their standard of living was much higher than most of the Africans around them, but there was no breath of creativity or beauty in their homes, and thus nothing welcoming or comforting or hospitable in their surroundings. And it was this lack of physical hospitality that spoke louder to these African young men than any sermons the missionaries might have preached. Can you see that it's not only our hearts which need to be hospitable, but our houses as well?

I was discussing this idea with a friend one day, and he was having a difficult time with my assertions. He insisted that God cares about what's in our hearts, and we don't need to worry about things like external beauty, as long as there is internal beauty. "Your problem is that you're a radical cosmological dualist," I said to my friend. "Is it terminal?" he replied with a grin on his face. "No," said I, "but it can definitely be crippling in terms theology; and if you have a crippled theology, you will have a crippled life." I did not return the grin, and my friend began to get the point that I was very serious about the issue, and so he became serious as well.

The reason I am so serious about this subject is that radical cosmological dualism is a way of looking at the world which is very commonly held by believing Christians, and from a Biblical perspective it is an absolutely false view of life. And this false view of life is one of the very powerful reasons that the Christian faith exerts an ever shrinking influence for good in Western culture, and in the world at large.

Consider the following; in the fine arts and in the cinema in this first half of the 21st century, the Christian faith has almost no influence. Can you think of any artists or film makers who are known for their Christian point of view, or for a message of godliness that their work articulates? What about in the fields of science, or mathematics, or economics, or education? Or have you heard of influential people who are known for putting revolutionary and transforming ideas to work in the business world specifically from a Biblical perspective? During a presidential election you may hear candidates assert that their Christian faith is a primary motivating factor in their lives, but have you ever heard them articulate policy that has a direct connection to that faith? In that same context, we who try to integrate our faith with our politics are constantly bombarded with the phrase "the Constitutional principle of the separation of church and state." This is an effort to get Christians to shut up about a Biblical perspective in the world of politics, and it has had the effect of emasculating the power of Christianity to accomplish good in a culture, relegating faith to a small and very private corner of life. But did you know that the phrase "separation of church and state" is not in the Constitution? All of these things relate to the fact that radical cosmological dualism has been doing its insidious work, eating away at a full and robustly Biblical view of the world for centuries. And many of us who are believing Christians are unaware of this erosion, and at times are even unwitting accomplices in its destructive effects.

So what is this terrible thing called radical

cosmological dualism? It sounds pretty heady. Does it really have any practical effect in life, or is it only something debated in the ivory towers of academe?

Well, to begin with, there are many dualisms, some of which describe an accurate view of life from a Biblical perspective. For example, the Bible asserts that there is such a thing as moral dualism, or more accurately moral dualities. In this view there is an absolute difference between right and wrong in the realm of morals. But this moral dualism often gets confused and mixed up with cosmological dualism in which the universe is divided into two completely separate realms – the secular and the sacred. And these two realms are made up of the material and the immaterial respectively. In addition, these two realms are seen as evil and good respectively. So, the secular and the material are evil, or at least unimportant, and the sacred and immaterial are good and valuable. One way this cosmological dualism works out in practicalities is seen very clearly in the way so many Christians talk about "ministry," or "full time Christian service," as the most spiritual of possible occupations – in contrast to just about any other "secular" job which is seen as less spiritual, and thus less important and less meaningful in the great scheme of things. In the same way, the arts are seen as a worldly pursuit, unless the artist is producing particularly "Christian" art – which usually amounts to pretty but rather insipid pictures with Bible verses tacked on them. In this dualistic cosmology God isn't interested in the cinema, or theatre, or music, science, education, technology, medicine or politics; and much less is he interested in such things as home building, or craftsmanship, or interior design. These are seen as things we must do in order to make enough money to pay the bills while waiting to die and go to heaven. But the more we can give ourselves to Bible study, and prayer, and church-going, and evangelism – the more we have invested in things of eternal value and significance, and the less we have wasted our lives. It's the idea that if I must be a business man rather than a pastor, at least I can make it a Christian business by offering Bible study at lunch time. All these things describe an emphatically unbiblical and false view of life, but are points of view widely held among evangelical, Bible believing Christians.

The Biblical view, on the other hand, is quite refreshingly and wonderfully different! The truth is that there is no such dualistic separation between the material and the spiritual. There is a difference, but it is quantitative and not qualitative. After all, God created the material world, and pronounced it "very good." (Genesis 1.31) And even though the creation is now fallen, it is still substantially good. The Bible says that the material world, even in its fallen state, declares the glory of God and displays his handiwork. (Psalm 19.1) The creative power, intelligence, artistic genius, and incomparable competence of God are all seen in his material creation, and the first task he gave us in the Garden of Eden was to interact intimately with that creation. In fact it is that very interaction which results in commerce and culture – things which so many Christians think of as intrinsically "worldly." Further, God's interest in, and commitment to the material world is seen ultimately in the incarnation of Jesus. The Son of God, the second Person of the Trinity, became a real flesh and blood man, and it is as a flesh and blood man that he was crucified and rose from the dead – and yes, even ascended to heaven. Since the Incarnation, there is and ever will be a man in the Godhead – with hair on his arms and the ability to eat and drink real physical food.

Again, in terms of practicalities, this means that God is interested in things like science. He cares about medicine, and education, and farming, and architecture, and auto mechanics. If Jesus is Lord of all, it means he is Lord of quantum physics and plumbing, as well as heaven and the heavenly host. All these things are important to God, and thus worthy of our time and attention. Work is actually a sacred thing, whether it is in the ministry, or in the grocery store. As a Christian then, the issue is not so much *what* I do, as *how* I do it. For instance, what makes a contractor a *Christian* contractor is not how many Bible studies he has during lunch with his crew, or how many clients he leads to Christ. Although those things are perfectly fine, it's not the tacking on of certain activities that are seen as sacred, which makes his work "Christian." Rather, it is his commitment to excellence and integrity *in the work itself,* in order to serve the client and bring glory to God – that makes the difference. Looking at it from a Biblical point of view, I am to see *the work itself as sacred,* and thus meaningful and with the potential to reflect positively on God, whom I represent in my work.

Now I imagine, by this time, you're wondering if this chapter was meant for an altogether different book, and something got mixed up at the printers. What has radical cosmological dualism got to do with hospitality, and particularly with the idea of the hospitable house?

To illustrate what I'm getting at let's look together at a rather obscure pair of gentlemen from the Old Testament, Bezalel and Oholiab.

> [1] Then the LORD said to Moses,
> [2] "See, I have chosen Bezalel son of Uri, the son of Hur, of the tribe of Judah,
> [3] and I have filled him with the Spirit of God,

with skill, ability and knowledge in all kinds of crafts--
[4] to make artistic designs for work in gold, silver and bronze,
[5] to cut and set stones, to work in wood, and to engage in all kinds of craftsmanship.
[6] Moreover, I have appointed Oholiab son of Ahisamach, of the tribe of Dan, to help him. Also I have given skill to all the craftsmen to make everything I have commanded you:
[7] the Tent of Meeting, the ark of the Testimony with the atonement cover on it, and all the other furnishings of the tent--
[8] the table and its articles, the pure gold lampstand and all its accessories, the altar of incense,
[9] the altar of burnt offering and all its utensils, the basin with its stand-
[10] and also the woven garments, both the sacred garments for Aaron the priest and the garments for his sons when they serve as priests,
[11] and the anointing oil and fragrant incense for the Holy Place. They are to make them just as I commanded you." (Exodus 31:1-11)

There is quite a lot written in the New Testament about spiritual gifts, and over the last few decades there has been a great deal of renewed interest in what they are and how they function. But here in Exodus 31 we have the very first mention of spiritual gifts in the Bible. Note the nature of them and what they were given for. They were special abilities or enablings from the Holy Spirit in order to be skilled in designing and executing jewelry, metal work, wood work, and beautiful and high quality fabrics for clothing. Think of it; the first spiritual gifts were given to produce excellence in the worlds of architecture, interior design, jewelry and fashion! This should put to flight any sense that these things are intrinsically worldly, evil, unspiritual, materialistic, or less important to God than things like Bible study and evangelism. Bezalel and Oholiab show us that God cares about skillful and beautiful craftsmanship in the things we make, just as he cares about them in the things he made.

I have heard many Christians express the sentiment that caring about beauty is a worldly and materialistic concern and something to be avoided, just as we should avoid greed and idolatry and lust. But here again is the mixing of moral dualism with cosmological dualism. The desire to create something beautiful is not intrinsically evil. In fact, it is an impulse that comes from being made in the image of God. If God cares about beauty and quality in the material world, so should we. When we pray "Thy Kingdom come; thy will be done on earth as it is in heaven," it is very instructive on this issue. Heaven is not going to be a squalid and ugly place. Neither is it going to be a mediocre and insipid place. Every square inch of it will be filled with beauty. It will be skillfully and wonderfully made in its architecture, its landscape, its art and its craftsmanship. And if it is God's will for heaven to be like that, then surely it is his will for earth to be the same; "...Thy will be done on earth as it is in heaven." So we who believe in him are to be the agents of that will on earth. We are to have a commitment to God's will being done on earth as it is in heaven, not only in the area of morals, but in every area of life.

God is the ultimate artist, and since we are made in his image we have those same creative impulses. A Christian then, above all people, should live artistically, aesthetically, and creatively. After all, we represent the Creator. The fact that you are a Christian should show up in practical areas of your life, and particularly in a growing creativity and sensitivity to beauty, rather than in a gradual drying up of creativity, and a blindness to ugliness.

So to reiterate my point, this chapter is about hospitality and its relationship to beauty in the external, material world, and that there is a connection between the internal and external.

Dualism says there is no connection. Biblical Christianity says the two are an integrated whole. We must have a hospitable heart in order to be hospitable to others, but we must also have a hospitable house. The physical place we live has a very important role to play in the way we express hospitality. I know that this particular idea may be very difficult for some Christians to embrace. It may even make you mad. Maybe you've been taught all your life that the material world doesn't matter to God…that it's what's in your heart that matters. And, of course, to a great extent that is true. You may have the most hospitable house in the world, but if you don't have a hospitable heart it will all be useless in the Kingdom of God. In fact, that is the reason I've spent most of the time in this book emphasizing that very point. But it would be wrong, and present a false view of hospitality, if we were to avoid looking, with careful theology, at the very real importance of creativity, and physical artistic beauty in the exercise of hospitality.

PHYSICAL EXPRESSIONS OF HOSPITALITY

So, when it comes to your home, what can you do to make it hospitable? Does it need to look like something on the cover of Traditional Home or Architectural Digest? Definitely not. But it is important to understand that whether or not you care about interior design, you have already done interior design. If the rooms you live in are slovenly, or sterile, or devoid of anything creative, *that* is your interior design. *That* is what you have created – *that* is the environment you have produced for you and your family, if you have one, to live in. Conversely, if you have thought about a seating arrangement that is conducive to conversation, and about lighting that is soothing, and about something interesting to artfully hang on your walls – then you have worked on the interior design of your home in a way that will speak hospitably to you, and anyone else who might come along.

In practical terms then, let me give you a handful of suggestions to consider as you think about making your house a reflection of God's hospitable heart, and of course your hospitable heart as well. I make these suggestions with the understanding that not all of them will apply to each of you, but I hope you will find some of them meaningful and helpful.

So let's start with you. *You* are valuable enough to live in a hospitable home, whether it is a large house, or a small apartment, or a room you are renting in someone else's house. When he created the heavens and the earth, God went to a great deal of trouble to put together a beautiful and hospitable place for you to inhabit. And if you are worth it to him, then you should honor what he values, and be worth it to yourself. So take some time, energy, creativity, and yes, even some money if possible, to make your home hospitable.

There is some truth to the old proverb that "cleanliness is next to godliness." Heaven will not be a messy place, and neither should your house be. The idea is that a hospitable house is a clean house. Don't be obsessive – we're not aiming at perfection but at comfort and welcome. Fold and put away clothes. Throw away garbage. Vacuum the floors, clean the toilets, and dust the furniture. If you're not used to doing this it takes a little work and discipline, but it's worth the effort. Your house will be more hospitable because you will feel more comfortable and welcome in your own home, and so will any who might visit you. But I'm encouraging you to do this not only when you're having guests in, but on a regular basis. It is an important way to be hospitable to yourself. Creating an environment that is neat and orderly rather than chaotic is a very worthwhile endeavor hospitality-wise. It will nourish your soul because your home will welcome you and others in a physical way.

Another important basic is that a hospitable house requires a dedicated space for guests. I have a bachelor friend who lives in his own three bedroom house, and his living room is furnished with various and sundry exercise and weight machines. He asked me for some advice about his house, so I encouraged him to get the gymnasium out of his living room. Since he has three bedrooms, he can use one for an office, a second for exercise, and the third for an actual bedroom. When he struggled with my suggestion I told him that maybe there's a reason people tend to demur when he invites them to his home. There is really no place of welcome for them – no place of beauty to just sit and have a conversation and a meal. He didn't need to buy new furniture, or re-carpet the floors. For starters, he just needed to neaten up the place, and move the Nautilus equipment. For my friend, hospitality had to become as high a priority as exercise.

As you're thinking about how your house can accommodate hospitality, think about function. I have a relative (name withheld to protect the guilty) who has an all-white living room. The carpet, the upholstery, the drapes, the tables, and even the grand piano are white. And believe it or not, it is a very lovely room. But when another relative ventured to actually sit on the sofa, they were quickly disabused of the notion, and led into the family room where the furniture was, in fact, allowed to be used. Clearly, the function of the all-white living room was

as something to look at but not touch, and thus was
rather lacking in its sense of welcome. If, on the
other hand, the intended function of your living
room, or family room, is to share life with people, it
might be wise to take a different approach.
Remember, if you want your upholstered furniture
to be comfortable and welcoming it's a good idea to
choose fabrics that can be easily cleaned so that the
inevitable splash of red wine is no big deal. And for
me, I like my guests to feel free to put their feet up
on the coffee table, so I try to use something that
doesn't mind getting another scratch on it. Again,
thinking about function, chairs and a sofa facing
each other around a coffee table is much more
conducive to human interaction and conversation
than everything pointed at the TV. Another thing
that helps make a room function hospitably is to
have, to the extent possible, some kind of table and
lamp by each chair or seating area. This gives you
and your guests a place to rest your coffee cup or
dessert plate, and provides soft and comfortable
lighting. Speaking of lighting, lamps are very
important. Ceiling fixtures are great in the kitchen,
but tend to be harsh, garish, and too bright in other
rooms, unless they are on a dimmer. And even if
you have them dimmed, lamps are still very
important to bring soft light welcomingly into a
room. Lamps can also be a fun and creative way to
express your own taste and individuality. But the

point of all these suggestions is to help you consider thoughtfully how each useful object in a room can be employed in a way that makes people feel welcome, relaxed and at home.

Since we're considering the role of function, and since hospitality often takes place around a meal, we need to think about the importance of your dining room. Not all houses have a dining room, to be sure. Many small apartments only have a bar that extends from the kitchen counter, and if you live in a rented room you may be used to eating dinner on the end of your bed while watching TV. But whether you have an old fashioned cavernous dining room that can accommodate 20 people, or live in a tiny studio apartment, the importance of a place where two or more people can sit together and share a meal cannot be over-estimated. Your dining room is the place where much of your hospitality will happen, and with a little ingenuity almost anyone can create such a hub of hospitality.

Many folks have a dining room that is rarely if ever used. It might have a lovely dining table and 8 chairs and sport a silk flower arrangement in the middle of the table with candles on either side that are never lit. It often has a buffet or hutch packed with beautiful china, crystal, silver, and linen napkins; lovely things which rarely if ever emerge from their safe cocoon of neglect. You can probably tell by my tone that I deplore the unused state of the American dining room. It is symbolic of the sad state of hospitality in the American church, and a loss of appreciation for all the beauty that can occur around a meal thoughtfully prepared and artfully presented. Let me urge you then, if you are fortunate enough to have an actual dining room, to please begin to make use of it! For starters, why not, once a week, plan to have the family eat in the dining room instead of in front of the TV in the family room? It doesn't have to be a big production – just a change of venue. And why not, every month or two, plan to have a few guests over for a meal that actually *is* a big deal. Get out the china and the linen napkins and make something memorable for friends and strangers – to serve them and give them something special, and to enjoy a holy time of building loving relationships.

I understand that not everyone can do this. As I said, not everyone has a dining room. But even if you live in a studio apartment, you could put up a card table, or use a small round end table; cover it with a table cloth; put a handful of tulips in a simple vase; add a candle or two, and use the best dishes you have. If all you have is paper plates, no problem, put them to use in reaching out hospitably. Just do it as creatively and beautifully as you can with what you have, and with what you can afford. If you only have paper plates but can afford dishes, get them. Pier 1, Pottery Barn, Crate and Barrel, Target…there are dozens of places that offer rich and creative ways to make a beautiful environment for your guests at minimal cost. Or what about garage sales, and tag sales, and estate sales?

Another idea to keep in mind is that color can influence hospitality. The color or colors that you paint a room have a powerful effect on the feel of that room, but there is no wrong or right color. It must be something that, first and foremost, welcomes *you*. If you are comfortable with the color, then your family and guests will likely follow suit. But, let me dispel one myth about color. Most people feel like white, or off-white will make a room feel lighter and larger. Although this is sometimes true, white tends to feel cold, and if you live in a gray climate will feel very gray and dreary. By all means, use white if you love it, but feel free to consider a soft buttery yellow, or a mellow sage green if you want to bring a light and lively feeling into a room. Also, consider a relaxed approach to the way you mix colors. Don't be too worried about whether one color goes with another. Don't fret or agonize that one shade of green might clash with another shade of green. Look at a garden and observe how God mixes colors quite lavishly, take courage, and try something a little unorthodox if you want to. The most important factor in mixing color, texture, and pattern is whether or not you love it. If you do, it will probably work, be welcoming, and make you and your guests feel at home.

In making your home hospitable, consider the idea that objects are important. By objects, I mean the things beyond lamps and furniture that provide interest, beauty, and personality to your house. These include things like pictures, collections, sculpture, plants, flowers, books, sea shells, ceramics and textiles. These are the things that give soul and personality to a home, that reflect your unique taste, and display your interests. My grandmother was a professor of art at the University of California Santa Barbara. Grandma Ruth loved to travel, and wherever she went she brought home wonderful and interesting things that she displayed beautifully in her house. There were antique Samurai swords and pre-Columbian huacos. (Water jars in the shape of strange animals and fantastic beings.) There were 18th century carved wooden boxes from Europe, and beautiful silk textiles from Thailand. Cambodian temple carvings and Japanese netsuke (tiny sculptures of incredible skill and detail) shared space on her book case with Guatemalan folk sculptures and a small carved replica of a butterfly boat from Lake Pazcuaro. She loved and appreciated the artistic expressions and skilled craftsmanship from cultures around the world, and caused me to catch a similar disease. I too am an inveterate collector and have many of Grandma Ruth's things displayed in my house, along with other things my wife and I have found on travels and adventures – each with its own story and memory. Becky loves sea shells and I love leather books; she loves lacy linens and I love antique santos (carvings of various Catholic saints) – and they all mix together in our home in a way that draws people in, welcomes them, and creates an environment that is filled with beauty and interest.

Objects are usually of no "practical" value...that is, they can't be used, like a screw driver, or a frying pan to accomplish some task. But you could say the same thing about the beautiful rainbow-like finish on the inside of an abalone shell, or the plumage on a peacock, or the awe-inspiring colors of orange and coral and purple that flash across the sky during a sunset over the Santa Rosa vineyards. They are of no practical value – if you don't believe that nourishing the soul is practical. They are of no practical value if beauty is meaningless and art is a waste of time. They are useless if the enrichment of life and of human experience is superfluous. But I think that Bezalel and Oholiab tell us a different story. They show that God himself is interested in man interacting with the raw materials he provided in order to create something beautiful. However imperfect, it's an inclination that flows from all people because we are made in the image of God, and it's part of the wonder of being human. And the thing about objects in your home, whether collected or made yourself, is that they speak uniquely of you. Some people like many, some like very few. Some like modern and some like old. Big or small, rustic or refined, simple or complicated, I would encourage you to consider that they are an important part of what makes your house hospitable.

The point of these suggestions is that God gave Bezalel and Oholiab special gifts for designing and decorating and skillfully creating a tabernacle - a physical "house" that was meant to represent his presence on earth. That being the case, shouldn't we take the same care and thoughtfulness in the way we represent him with our own houses? Don't let radical cosmological dualism lead you to the wrong conclusion – that these physical things don't matter – that it's only the internal, immaterial, "spiritual" part that matters. How many other people, like those young African university students who were raised with a sensitivity to beauty, are chased away from the Christian faith because we misrepresent the Great Artist as a God who has little use for these unimportant things. Our very homes can and do preach loudly about our view of God because they are so linked to the way we practice hospitality.

Just last week we had new friends over for dinner. We have known Dennis and Jan for about a year, and have had several occasions to engage in serious conversation with them about our lives and theirs – about what is important to us, what God is doing in us, and what he may want to do through us. But they lead very busy lives, constantly traveling around the country and the world, so this was the first time they were free to come to dinner. Dennis, who is not one to wax lyrical about such things, was fascinated by our little place. Referring to an antique santo I had made into a lamp, he said "I have never seen such an interesting lamp." And he had similar comments about much of the other "stuff" in our house. But what was most significant to me about his observations was when he said "I know you in a completely different way now that I've been in your home." The house you live in, whether you're intentional about it or not, speaks volumes about who you are. It puts on display what is interesting and important to you – your likes and dislikes – your strengths and weaknesses. The point of this chapter then, is that if hospitality is valuable to you, understand and make use of your house as a very significant tool in practicing this important grace.

As God's hospitable heart is growing in your heart,

don't allow a dualistic world view to sever the linkage in your life between the material world and how you help people feel at home. Find ways to express to others the same welcome that God holds out to you, through the physical thing that is your house. Whether it's a comfortable chair, a cozy dining room, a creative arrangement of art on your walls, or a collection of sea shells on your mantle – all these objects in the physical world play an important part in expressing welcome and comfort to those people whom God brings within the orbit of your life.

XI. THE CONVIVIUM

I hope I have helped you see the idea of hospitality in a new light. I have tried to show that the essence of hospitality is not just knowing how to put on a dinner. It is not just recipes and decorations and seating charts and guest lists. And it certainly is not the same thing as our modern notion of "entertainment". Entertainment, when it is used in the context of hospitality, tends to carry with it the idea of social obligation and the need to impress. It is often putting my best foot forward in order to curry favor with someone who can, in return, procure some advantage for me. On the other hand hospitality, in its biblical form, is a perspective on life - a posture toward people - an orientation of the heart. In fact, hospitality is a word that describes something essential in the character of God. True hospitality is a grace that springs from God, and is manifested through his children in the form of an open, out-going, welcoming love of, care for, and curiosity about people.

But having said all that, and with the understanding that real hospitality begins and ends with a heart full of love toward people, I think we are now ready to talk about hospitality in terms of practicalities - to take concrete steps toward experiencing the serious adventure of hospitality.

Have you ever gone to a restaurant by yourself? And do you remember if you felt awkward just sitting there staring into space waiting for your meal to come? And when it did come, did you feel like something was missing as you ate in solitude? And did you think to yourself "I'm never going to do this again. If I ever eat by myself in the future, I'm going to at least have a book to read or a crossword puzzle to do because eating alone is just not the way things were meant to be." There's something much better about eating a meal in the company of others than by yourself. In fact, to me, one of life's saddest sights is seeing someone sitting alone in a restaurant, eating by himself. It makes me feel in a visceral way that there is something fundamentally wrong - that human beings were not made to eat alone. It's like rubbing salt into that fundamental woundedness of man - that loss of home that we feel when we're alone and isolated. It can exacerbate that sense of living in a hostile and inhospitable world when we sit by ourselves and eat alone.

In sharp contrast, nothing could be more hospitable than sharing a meal with others. Let me give you a recent example; last week my wife Becky and I were invited to have Saturday brunch with friends in their back yard. I asked if there was anything we could bring and they said "If it's not too much trouble, could you bring those wonderful scones you make?" I said we'd be glad to, and we also brought orange juice and champagne for mimosas. After all, what's a Saturday brunch without mimosas!? (I'm just sayin').

It was a lovely, sunny morning, about 75 degrees. The picnic table was beautifully set with a big bowl of fruit and berries, unbreakable picnic plates and glasses (since our friends have four young children), bottles of fizzy things to drink, delicious eggs wrapped in bacon, a basket full of our fantastic - if I do say so myself - orange cranberry scones, and of course the makings for mimosas. When I started to un-cork the champagne our host Adam said to his son Zorin "I bet Mr. Mike can make that cork shoot really high up in the sky." Thus liberated, I pointed the bottle in the direction of the neighbor's house and it flew well over the fence. Zorin thought I was awesome. Adam said "We have a good relationship with the neighbors - they have returned many baseballs to us, but this will be the first champagne cork."

We sat down, held hands and thanked God for the food asking him to bless our time together, and then we dug in. Water was spilled by children several times, once drenching my right pants-leg, but there was never an angry retort or an impatient sigh. When I was a child something spilled was a fairly major faux pas - voices were raised - tears were shed. I felt myself envious of children with such patient parenting, and guilty that I didn't show such patience with my children. Much can be learned around a dinner table with friends and their children … and in unexpected ways, and from surprising sources. Conversation flowed freely as we talked about children and grandchildren; painting an old dresser from the Salvation Army to make it beautiful for our twin grandbabies 6th birthday; new friends from church and what their needs are and how we can befriend them; how to deal with people who are demanding and judgmental; can a chiropractor help you with your migraine headaches; the theological significance of Jesus' encounter with Zaccheus, etc. etc. The kids had long since run off to play on the trampoline and our conversation continued to run the gamut from the mundane to the meaningful. At one point I found myself telling the story of a trip to Mexico that Becky and I took on our 30th anniversary. It was a funny experience involving scorpions at the dinner table, and I tend to get rather dramatic when telling a story, including whatever ethnic accent that might come into play. The story ends with Federico, our very gracious matre d' assuring us that "Oh no senor, it was not a scorpion, but only a much smaller and less dangerous creature. If you are stung by the scorpion, you will DIE. But if you are stung by this creature, I can assure you, you will not die, it will only damage you." As I finished the story Adam pointed out that all the kids had quietly returned to the table and were listening intently to find out what happened with the scorpion. I don't think they saw the humor in being "only damaged" by a smaller bug, but they were certainly enthralled. Then their dad asked if any of the kids had a story they would like to share, and each one had some tale of adventure to offer. So we spent the rest of the morning and into the early afternoon listening to narratives of camping adventures, Disneyland adventures, and tall tales of the imagination.

As you can see, nothing earth-shattering or dramatically significant happened at this Saturday brunch with friends. But there is a sub-text running through this experience that must not be overlooked or you will miss the importance of this kind of interaction. Friendships were growing; affection was being expressed; loyalties were being cemented; love was happening; community was being experienced. You need to know that we have only lived in Santa Rosa, California for just over a year, having moved from Seattle where we lived for 40 years. We moved to a place where we didn't know a soul, from a community in which many significant relationships had been forged over many decades. And the couple we were brunching with is 20 years younger than we. But because of their hospitality, their willingness to open their hearts and home to us and to share a meal with an older couple they barely know, they and several other families are making us feel at home. They are melting the feeling of isolation, and removing the sense of loneliness and the stigma of being invisible. When you move to a new and unfamiliar place, the ancient wound of the loss of home can be felt in an exceptionally strong way. But a simple meal with new friends can have a powerful and healing effect on that wound.

I know I've said that hospitality is not just about putting on a nice dinner, and yet here I am talking about "the friendly feast." That's because even though hospitality isn't *only* about a shared meal, the fact is that the shared meal is nevertheless one of the most powerful vehicles to express hospitality.

So why is this? Why is it that when we think about hospitality most of us tend to think of guests in our home, and an event usually centering on some kind of a special meal? Isn't it because hospitality is about welcoming someone and including them in a shared life? And what better place to share life than at the dinner table? In sharing a meal, you are giving valuable gifts to someone. First, you are sharing food. You must not underestimate the value of this gift. When you, with generosity and thoughtfulness share food with someone, you are satisfying one of the most basic of human needs, and interacting with one of the most fundamental of human pleasures. People love to gather for a feast because they love to eat good food - it's as simple as that!

But second, you are also sharing *yourself*, and this is an even more basic human need and human pleasure. When you share a meal with others there's conversation, interaction, the give and take of thoughts and ideas, likes and dislikes, hopes and dreams, jokes and stories. It's the exchange of life and the enhancement of relationships; and because loving a person starts with knowing him, a meal together is a wonderful opportunity for the cultivation of love.

In addition to that, feasting together is a celebration. It is the enjoying together of friendship; it is a way to revel in another person; it is a vehicle to extol an achievement, or memorialize a special event; it is the process of jubilation about anything or anyone worthy of our attention and remembrance.

When you think about it, the dynamic potential around a shared meal is shockingly potent, because it connects so fundamentally to the meaning of being human. It is the wonderful combination of the nourishment of body and soul. So, when you practice hospitality by inviting someone into your home for a meal, you are participating in something sacred, mysterious, and powerful. It involves being vulnerable enough with another person, trusting enough, to risk opening your life, your heart, and your home to them. What could be a more compelling expression of a welcoming heart of hospitality?

And of course we see this happening throughout the Bible. A shared meal was the focal point of hospitality in Biblical culture, both in the Old and New Testaments.

In (Genesis 18.1-8) Abraham eagerly invites three passing strangers to dine with him. A great deal of expense and energy is expended for the sake of the strangers because that is the expression of godly hospitality.

In (Genesis 24.17-33) Abraham's servant was sent to find a wife for Isaac. It was in the context of a shared meal that the servant was able to discover a suitable wife for his master's son.

When Moses rescued Reuel's daughters from some unscrupulous shepherds and the daughters reported the incident to their father, the father was incredulous that they had not invited the stranger to dinner. He immediately ordered them to do so, and Moses' journey toward finding a wife started at that meal. (Exodus 2.15-21.)

In the New Testament we see that the shared meal had just as important a place in the life of God's people – if not more so. In fact, in his great little book entitled A Meal With Jesus, Tim Chester points out that the shared meal was significantly central to Jesus' interaction with people. In (Luke 7.34) it says "The son of man has come eating and drinking…" This is a description, against all expectation, of the *way* Jesus came. The Jews of Jesus' day would be looking for the Messiah to come in power and glory, to bring justice and execute vengeance on the enemies of God. But the Bible says no, he came eating and drinking. And Jesus was not half-hearted about it either. He was so into the practice that his enemies accused him of being a glutton and a drunkard. He spent a great deal of time at meals with a diverse mix of people. In fact it can be said without exaggeration that in the entire gospel of Luke Jesus is either going to a meal, is at a meal, or is coming from a meal. And what we learn from this is that the shared meal was a primary focus of Jesus' strategy. It was around festive banquets that stretched long into the evening that Jesus engaged people, discipled them, and discussed and demonstrated the good news of the Kingdom of God. (Tim Chester; A Meal With Jesus; Crossway, Wheaton Illinois, 2011; P.11-12)

In (Luke 5.29-39), after calling Matthew the tax collector to be one of his disciples, Jesus is invited to a grand banquet at his house. There the Pharisees criticized Jesus for hanging out with "sinners," and Jesus masterfully exploded their religious self-righteousness. Jesus loved to have dinner with sinners. He explained that just as it is not healthy people who need a doctor, but sick people, so it is not righteous people who need a savior, but "sinners." Matthew's friends were an unsavory lot; but Jesus was showing that the hospitality of God is most appropriate in that context because those are the people most open to God's welcome since they see their need for Him.

In (Luke 10.38-42) Jesus is invited to dinner at the home of Mary and Martha, where we learn that hospitality can be a lot of work! (More on this later.)

In (John 2.1-11) Jesus performs his first miracle at a wedding banquet; he has dinner with Zacchaeus in Lk.19, with Simon the leper in Mk. 14, a Pharisee in Lk.7, and a chief Pharisee in Lk.14.

Significantly, the last meal Jesus shared with his disciples was the Passover Seder. This was a feast that God himself instituted to commemorate that night in Egypt when he sent the last plague that took the lives of all the firstborn of Egypt, because Pharaoh's heart was hard and he would not let God's people go. But on that same terrible night the children of Israel were sequestered in their homes, and it was on the doorposts and lintels of those homes that the blood of a lamb was sprinkled. When the angel of death passed through the land of Egypt that night, he passed over each home he saw sprinkled with the blood, safe from the awful plague that Pharaoh had brought upon his people. And it was the very next day that Pharaoh changed his mind and let God's people go out from Egypt, freed from their bondage to slavery. So this was the commemorative meal that Jesus was celebrating with his disciples just before his crucifixion, and it is in memory of that same feast and all its New Covenant meaning that the church celebrates Holy Communion. The Communion feast is the affirmation that the meaning of Passover was fulfilled in Jesus, because through his blood shed on the cross, God passes over our sins, as we sit huddled in His house, freed from the penalty of death.

So we can see, in the Bible, it is around a meal that life is so often shared. It is there that lessons are taught, presuppositions clarified and challenged, friendships formed and strengthened, regrets expressed and forgiven, understandings gained, covenants made, healing begun, community experienced. Thus the richness of life and the heart of hospitality are often shared around these convivial feasts. In fact the very word "convivial" gives us insight into the subject. The English word *convivial* is based the Latin *convivium*, for a feast or banquet. More broadly it means life together, from *con (with)* + *vivio (living)*. In fact, in Latin the Eucharist is called "Sanctum Convivium." But I think it's fascinating that recently - since the early 1990's - the word convivium has become part of the English-speaking world and is used to refer to groups that gather together for good food and friendly conversation.

So even embedded in our language is the idea that hospitality and conviviality are tied together, and that one of the most appropriate contexts to experience that hospitality is the shared feast, banquet, meal…the convivium.

Specifically what this looks like will differ with each person, couple, or family that seeks to practice hospitality at home. Just as God has created and gifted each person uniquely, so the way you practice hospitality will take on the special flavor of who you are. But we also learn from and inspire each other, so I want to give you an idea of what the "convivium" looks like for my wife Becky and me.

Imagine peeking into the window of our little apartment on an evening we shared with new friends when we first moved to California. What you see is a true story, and fairly typical of how dinner with us would look…surely not every night, but on those special nights when we invite guests to share with us.

So, are you're ready? Let's invite someone to dinner!

Candles are lit, the lights are dim, and soft music is playing in the background. The most enticing, saliva-producing, romance-evoking aromas are filling our apartment. I had been cooking all day. A "crustade de coq au vin" – French style chicken in wine sauce – is gurgling happily in the oven. The rich dark mushroom, bacon, and onion studded sauce is bubbling through the puff pastry crust which is slowly turning a deep golden brown.

Becky has tossed pecan halves in butter and sugar on the stove. They will be added at the last minute to fresh organic greens and dried cranberries, sliced ripe pears, and Laura Chanel goat cheese, for our first course salad.

We are having company for dinner. Becky had set the table as soon as she got home from work. Our apartment dining room is small. It just fits an old oval iron table that looks like it belongs in a French bistro. We can seat six people, barely, but cozily. The table is set with a mix of antique dishes from my mom and grandmother, and the sterling silver is from Becky's family. The salad will go in the old Japanese rectangular imari dishes Grandma Ruth bought in post-war Japan, and the dinner dishes are a floral spray with a patterned green rim that belonged to my mother. We'll serve dessert on the antique fish plates, part of an old fish service we bought 30 years ago in Boston. Each plate has a different hand painted fish swimming in a greenish sea with flowering seaweed and coral. It's really a stunning mix that creates a beautiful table-scape, made all the more so because each dish carries a significant memory.

The large, creamy white napkins are from our collection of vintage linens, folded simply beside each plate. They are a complete pain to wash and iron, but they are so much more special to use than paper napkins, and I hope we are being at least a bit environmentally conscious.

Things are ready and our guests begin to arrive. We are having two couples from our new church. One couple brings us a large container of many-hued organic brown eggs. The other couple has a bottle of very special wine in hand.

I am happy. Becky is happy. This is what we love most to do together. Hospitality. Inviting friends, strangers, workmates into our home, feeding them the best we can afford, and loving them as best we know how. This all takes place around a table whose very essence tells them "You are special. You are worth going to a lot of trouble for."

I have pulled creamy hot toasted parmesan rounds from the broiler. Becky has poured the wine, red or white, or sparkling water, for each guest. We sit around the coffee table in our tiny living room. The conversation is a little slow and awkward at first, as these are new friends, but we ask questions about each other's lives, and begin to get an idea of each person's unique story. Soon everyone feels at ease because when we share about who we are, what we do, and what makes us mad and glad, it's easy to contribute. Plus my toasted parmesan rounds are a hit, and all our guests insist that I must find a way to commercially market them because "everyone would buy them."

By now it's time for the short journey (about 4 ½ feet) to the dining room. After savoring the salad, the coq au vin is transported from the kitchen (about 2 ½ feet away) and sits gloriously in the middle of the table, steaming its delicious aromas toward the nose of each guest. It is scooped out of its red-enameled iron pot with a huge spoon and ladled generously over homemade buttered noodles. (I don't always have time for homemade, but they're extra delicious so I make them when I can.) The candles flicker and reflect beautifully off the crystal and sterling silver. The conversation lags for a few minutes as we tuck in to the "coq". But soon we're re-engaged with each other as we enjoy good food, discover new friends, and share a convivial evening of hospitality together.

While this may describe a familiar experience that many of you have created in the exercise of hospitality, to others it may seem a bit out of reach…too fussy, and too much work, or too complicated a menu. But let me urge you to not be intimidated or put off by such things. As I said, each person or family will have their own unique way of expressing hospitality, and one way is not better than another as long as it is filled with love. So never fear! The purpose of this chapter is to inspire and give practical help. The important thing is not to compare yourself with someone else, but to dive in and simply do – take the plunge and have an adventure.

With that in mind, what I'd like to do in this section is give you some very practical suggestions about thought and preparation for a meal – why's and wherefores. Then at the end of the book I have provided an appendix which contains recipes for several shared meals, designed for the different kinds of opportunities that God gives you to practice hospitality. Many of you have done this kind of thing before, so it will be easy for you to glean some ideas, take whatever inspiration is here, and run with it. On the other hand, many of you may never have invited a group of people to your home for a meal. Perhaps, if you have a family, you seldom even have family dinners because each of you is running in twelve directions at once and you never seem to have a time when the whole family can gather together for an evening. (By the way - if this is your experience, I recommend watching a little movie called Uncle Nino. In a delightful way, it poignantly shows the importance of finding time for this vitally important part of life.) But whether you're a veteran or a novice at sharing a meal with guests and/or family, the ideas I give you here are just that - ideas to get you started; they are a place to begin or to re-ignite your foray into the realm of practicing hospitality, and the possibility of entertaining angels.

Let's start with some basic perspective:

Hospitality can be a lot of work.

In our culture of fast-food, and frozen dinners, and paper plates, and disposable cutlery, we are going to have to make a shift in our thinking. The purpose of hospitality is to take time, effort, and work to demonstrate to those you welcome that they are important enough and valuable enough for such an expenditure. Often the comments that my wife and I get when we welcome people for a meal are about how much our guests were made to feel special. And they usually explain that this is because it is obvious we worked hard and thought creatively and put a lot of love into the meal itself, as well as into the people attending the meal. And this is very gratifying to us because it is the fulfillment of our goal. We want people, as a result of our hospitality, to feel special, loved, important - that is, to experience how God feels about them. And as with anything in life, it takes some work to accomplish this significant goal. But it is not an un-welcome kind of work, because it's fun to be creative and to put effort into doing something special for somebody else. Since such an important task takes some thoughtful preparation, the following are some things to keep in mind as you work on this expression of God's Kingdom.

Thinking About a Menu

When you invite someone to a meal, you obviously need to **decide what you're going to eat**. You may have favorite recipes that you have made in the past, or maybe you want to try something new, but it takes some thought. There are almost limitless resources available to plan a menu. There are hundreds of cook books at Barnes and Noble, and thousands of recipes on line. But sometimes there is so much information that you can get buried in the deluge - which is why I am giving you a few simple ideas for starters. However, if you don't like my suggestions, feel free to look elsewhere…there's plenty to choose from! But don't agonize over what you're going to serve, just choose something you feel comfortable with and that you think your guests will enjoy. Also, it doesn't hurt to ask those you invite if they have any special dietary restrictions or foods they particularly dislike. I always appreciate it when someone asks me those questions because it gives me the chance to nix anything made with eggplant or cilantro. (Two exceptions I think God should have made when he declared all foods clean!!)

As you're thinking about what to serve, **keep in**

mind your own limitations. For instance, especially if you're new at hospitality, don't try to do something complicated. Delicious and thoughtful and beautiful doesn't always have to be complex or fussy.

Another thing to keep in mind is **your budget**. Welcoming people to dinner can be costly, and it is definitely worth it. Spending money on people to bring some love and joy and fellowship into their lives is not something any Christian should be hesitant to do…you're making an eternal investment, and you might be entertaining angels! But we all have our limitations. Some of us can afford steak and lobster, and some of us can only afford pasta. You know what is manageable for you budget-wise, and pasta is one of my favorite things to prepare for guests. But my exhortation is this; don't spend what you can't afford. Hospitality is not determined by how much you spend but by how much love you invest. On the other hand, don't begrudge doing something a little over the top if you can afford it. Think of the way God lavishes hospitality on us. Either way, exercise wisdom, and be as generous as you can.

A Time-frame

An additional aspect of thoughtful preparation is to understand **how much time** you will need. In my experience, when we have guests there are two essentially different types of meals. One is planned ahead, and one is last minute. Because of this, in the appendix I am giving you menu ideas for three planned-ahead meals where you can take the time and energy to put together something very special and carefully prepared. These meals are ones that can't be thrown together at the last minute. These are special events that you think about and give extra attention to for the sake of people you want to serve hospitably. They could even become a tradition that you want to incorporate into your life as part of the expression of hospitality that God is growing in your heart.

Specifically in terms of time, Becky and I try to have our menu planned about a week ahead of time where possible. We need to know what to get at the grocery store, and how much time it will take us to cook the meal. But we also need to include time for setting the table, straightening up the house, putting some flowers in a vase, and some candles in their place.

Now I know some of you are starting to think - "Wait a minute. You're a man, and you do flower arrangements, and house cleaning, and setting a table, and cooking a meal? Give me a break! There aren't many guys like you out there, and my husband doesn't care at all about some of these things." I know, I know. My wife and I share these responsibilities, and we love to do them together, and not every couple will be like us. And to be honest, early in our marriage I did almost no cooking, and very little setting of the table and caring about things like a flower arrangement. But as hospitality became more important to us, I became more involved in all aspects of it. So at least if you can get your husband to read this book and agree in principle that this whole hospitality thing is really important, then maybe, over time, he will be increasingly open to a deeper involvement with the nuts and bolts of accomplishing it.

But what about hospitality "on the run?" What about those circumstances where I run into someone unexpectedly and would love to have them to lunch or dinner? If I'm prepared for that to happen it is really no big deal, and makes for many fun and significant "conviviums." So with that in mind, the appendix also contains menu ideas for a handful of last minute meals that you can throw together quickly at the spur of the moment. But with regard to last minute hospitality, let me give you a few words of encouragement.

You might be one of those people who needs at least two weeks' notice before you would even consider having guests to dinner. My mother was this way, and it was because she wanted to be sure she had given the attention and preparation necessary to properly honor the guests she was inviting. However, often there is the sudden need or opportunity to be hospitable right now, and to wait for a more convenient time would be to miss the special thing God has in mind. Imagine if Abraham had said to the three men he saw approaching his tent in Genesis 18 "This week is really challenging, but if you could come back in two weeks when things are a little less crazy, I'd love to have you stay for dinner." If he hadn't been willing to practice hospitality "last minute", he would have missed out on one of the most pivotal experiences with God in his life.

So, while it is true that hospitality expressed by a shared meal deserves the time, and thought, and preparation that takes place over several days, or even weeks to create something very special, often God brings circumstances into our lives that call for more spontaneity. If we can prepare ahead for those kinds of experiences as well, we are free to practice hospitality at any moment.

In terms of spontaneous hospitality, I'm sure many of you have had experiences similar to what happened with me one Sunday morning just before church. I was walking through the room adjacent to the sanctuary when I noticed a young man I'd never seen before. He looked to be in his mid-20's, and he had his foot up on a chair tying the laces of a very unique-looking pair of black and white checkered tennis shoes. I thought "I've got to introduce myself to this guy because anyone who would wear black and white checkered tennies is going to be a very interesting person." So, I took the plunge, walked over to him, and introduced myself;

"I don't think I've seen you here before…my name is Mike, and those are really cool tennies."

"Hi Mike, my name's Greg; glad you like my shoes." (Big smile.)

Within minutes I discovered that Greg was new in town, recently graduated from college, and just starting a new job. He had been to one or two churches since he arrived in Seattle, and had heard about ours from a friend, so he thought he'd check it out. I told him I was really glad he had come, and invited him to sit with me in church - Becky had to work that morning so she couldn't join us - and that I'd be glad to "show you the ropes" of how to navigate through our particular church service, including important pieces of information like where to get coffee, and where to find the bathroom.

After church I could have said to this young man "Greg, it was great meeting you and I hope you'll come visit us again soon." We'd shake hands warmly, smile, and I'd probably never see him again. I could have thought to myself; "Maybe I should invite Greg and a couple of other folks from church to my house for lunch. But I've had a long week; I'm tired; I've got plans to work on some projects at home; and besides, what will I serve them for lunch? I haven't had any time to plan a menu, and I haven't even washed the dishes from breakfast this morning, so I'll just do my best to make Greg feel welcome at church, and pray that he'll come back when I'm more prepared and it's more convenient to be hospitable."

Now as I stated, I *could* have thought that way. But because I really believe in the value and importance and mandate of hospitality, I bagged all those excuses, some of which were very valid. Because hospitality is one of the primary ways God has given me to serve other people, I sometimes don't allow my excuses and busy-ness to get the upper hand. I'm willing to put off things like projects around the house when God gives me the opportunity to make a person feel welcomed and important...at least when I'm clothed and in my right mind.

So because of our commitment to hospitality, and in

order to help make spontaneous hospitality more easily accessible, Becky and I have done certain things ahead of time in preparation for those opportunities. We have a repertoire of menus that are specifically designed for last-minute gatherings. We try to keep our pantry stocked with the things those menus call for so we're ready at any moment to have a few folks over for a delicious lunch or dinner.

Because of that, and the grace of God, I didn't succumb to my excuses. I was happy to introduce Greg to Jacob - one of the young men I have had the privilege of mentoring over the last couple of years - and to invite the two of them home for lunch and conversation. The result of that decision was that Greg and I became fast friends, as did Greg and Jacob. God allowed me to become a mentor to Greg, helping him grow in his faith as he walks the precipitous path of following Jesus. And just recently I had the privilege of officiating at Greg's wedding to Jessica.

What a great experience! The gift of friendship and the enriching of life because of the unique and wonderful people God connects you to, are often the unexpected and surprising results of hospitality. And the hospitable meal (the convivium) is one of the primary vehicles through which these gifts of grace can be shared and cultivated.

Convivium; "With living." Sharing life with friends and strangers around a meal is very much at the heart of hospitality. Jesus "came eating and drinking," and so should we. It is in that context that we can express something of the depth of welcome that God has expressed to us in Jesus Christ. It is there we can say to the people who God brings into our lives that they *belong*. They are welcome to belong to us in friendship; they are encouraged to feel a sense of belonging to life and the world God created for them to live in as they are included in conversation and fellowship around something as rudimentary as meal together. And hopefully, through your hospitality, they will experience a taste of the mysterious and transcendent, as at that dinner years ago with Lynn and Della, where walls came down, fears dissipated, loneliness melted away, and a wandering human soul found his way back home.

INVITED HOME

XII. THE INHOSPITABLE CHURCH

It was the mid 1980's and I was on a trip through England and Scotland with a group of friends from several churches. We started in London, and one of the first places we went to see was Saint Paul's Cathedral. By any measure, Saint Paul's is one of the most spectacular church buildings in the world. It is the second largest – outdone in size only by the Vatican. It's great dome and cavernous spaces designed by Sir Christopher Wren are awe-inspiring and beautiful to behold. As such, it represents in inescapable, in-your-face physicality, something of the ancient Christian faith, to the millions of people who see and visit it every year. It says "If you come into this building, you are coming to a place designed to represent the Christian God." It is his house, and is meant to be a place where you experience something of who he is, and what he wants to communicate to the human race. And the building itself, in many wonderful ways, does just that through its awesome, majestic, creative, and beautiful architecture. But it is the people within that building – the ones who believe the message that the building represents – who have the responsibility to truly incarnate the good news of Jesus Christ.

It was late afternoon, and the church was filled with gawking tourists like me, staring up into the vast spaces enclosed by this great building, and reading the inscriptions on the many tombs and memorials enshrined within its walls. Up near the front of the church several hundred wooden folding chairs had been set up and roped off from the rest of the building. It was getting close to the time when the boys choir would enter and begin their wonderful service of singing, and this would take place while tourists continued their explorations. There were two priests in robes and clerical collar standing sentry at a gap in the rope. They would lift the rope and allow people who intended to stay for the service to enter the area and be seated. I decided to stay for the service, but apparently, as far as the priests were concerned, didn't fit the profile of someone who would be interested. So as I walked up to the rope the priests gave me a very cynical glance and said in a heavy London accent – "If you go in, you have to stay for the service." I said "Oh yes, I will stay for the service." Both priests rolled their eyes and as they begrudgingly lifted the rope for me to enter the seating area, one said to the other in a stage whisper meant to be heard by anyone listening... "Ten to one he doesn't stay!"

Well, of course I did stay, and was deeply moved by the sacred music sung by one of the greatest boys choirs in Western Civilization. But even though I have laughed about the experience many times since, I was actually offended and grieved by the off-putting and inhospitable spirit of those two Anglican priests who cared more about their rules of attendance than they did about the faith experience of a young man visiting their church from another country. What if I had been a non-believer? That single experience would be enough for many people to be turned off to the message of Jesus Christ for the rest of their lives. Sometimes, as Jesus' church, we do him a terrible disservice by the inconsiderate and inhospitable way we treat people who actually come in search of something real when they come to church.

One of the most telling bumper stickers I have ever seen, and unfortunately I've seen more than one of them, pleads "Jesus, save me from your people." This bumper sticker has caused me to sometimes laugh, and sometimes cry. I feel the humor of it, but

187

I also feel the serious indictment it is of God's people, the church, because of the inhospitable spirit we often express.

Of course the church is made up of individuals, and it is from the individual perspective I have approached most of this book, because I believe if individuals can be inspired to hospitality, then the church as a whole will benefit and become more hospitable. But it is also very important to see that the church is not just a collection of isolated individuals. The church is a community of interconnected individuals united under the headship of Jesus Christ. (Ephesians 4.7-16) Unfortunately that paradigm is often very poorly expressed and it is that poor expression which evokes the kind of bumper sticker I've just mentioned.

The thing about a united community is that its existence creates a more powerful expression of the ideas and values that animate its individual members. It's the classic example of the whole being greater than the sum of the individual parts. In our present context, the loving, welcoming heart of God is powerfully expressed through the hospitality of any individual who gives himself faithfully to its practice. But the power of that same welcoming embrace is increased exponentially when practiced by a community of believing people. But here's the rub;

it has been my observation that this principle cuts in both directions. A hospitable community is more powerful than a hospitable individual, but by the same token, an inhospitable community is more powerful than an inhospitable individual. Let me illustrate my point from two recent experiences.

Have you ever attended a church which was new to you and where you didn't know a soul? I can tell you that it is potentially a very intimidating and uncomfortable experience. This is true even for someone who has been around churches for many years, let alone for the person who is an outsider – a stranger to the faith perhaps, or someone who has been away from God for many years and is, with trepidation and timidity, seeking a way back. The reason for this discomfort is that a church is a community, and therefore is made up of people who are at least acquaintances if not friends. And when a stranger walks in to a group of people who already know each other well, the feeling of isolation is likely to be amplified. In addition to that, each church has its own way of doing things – whether it's the order of the service, the formality or informality of its approach to God, the general feeling of chatty friendliness or the quiet awe that characterizes that particular group. Even the choice of music and the way people dress are unique to each church. All these things can combine to make a person feel like a stranger in a strange land, and I have felt this way myself when I have visited unfamiliar churches. So, whether or not the church understands something of the power and significance of hospitality can make all the difference in the world to those venturing forth to get their feet wet in the Christian faith…not to mention members of the church who have been around for years and may still feel alone and isolated.

So come with me to a church (which shall remain nameless for obvious reasons) which I attended with my wife and my nine-year-old grandson last Easter. We were visiting our kids in Seattle at the time and ended up going to a church which was recommended by a friend. It is a fairly large church in the Seattle area, having experienced some steady growth over recent years, and with a new and much larger building to accommodate their congregation. Ever since I became a Christian, Easter has been very special to me since, for the first eighteen years of my life, I didn't know or believe there was such a thing as a resurrection. I love to celebrate the fact that death doesn't have the final word; that because Jesus was raised from the dead in space, time, and history, so will I be one day in the future. The resurrection changes everything! Life does not simply end in death, making everything absurd. Since life goes on forever and everything I do in this life has eternal consequences, there can be meaning and purpose even in the simple and mundane things of life.

As a result, Easter Sunday has great significance to me, and I love to celebrate with fellow Christians the fact that Jesus is risen, and to review in song sung and word preached the wonder of this keystone in the arch of the Christian faith. It has also been my experience that even among jaded Christians for whom so much of the faith is old hat, Easter Sunday still holds something very special – something worth celebrating and getting excited about. I was, because of that, anticipating with joy the experience of worshipping with brothers and sisters in Christ, even though I would be a stranger among them.

The parking lot was almost full – it was Easter after all – but we found a space and joined the crowd of people headed toward the sanctuary. There were young families, old folks, single adults and couples chatting with friends and looking for a place to sit. There were teenagers huddled in their little groups, and young kids chasing each other around in the foyer. And there were, stationed like sentries at the front door, the official "greeters" with a stack of church bulletins, and rather emphatic smiles. We nodded appreciatively as the greeter handed us a bulletin. I held on to BooBoo's hand, (that's my grandson's nickname), while Becky found a restroom. As BooBoo and I waited, sitting on a bench in the crowded foyer, I looked at people, wondering about their lives and about how the resurrection of Jesus had made a difference for them. I smiled at several folks who looked quickly away, not anxious to make eye contact with a stranger. Dozens of Bible-carrying people scurried by, preoccupied with one thing or another, but with never a look or a smile in our direction. I was beginning to feel invisible, but tried to ignore the feeling since it was Easter, Jesus is risen, and I'm going to be happy. Becky soon returned and we found our way to a seat in the sanctuary, not at the very back, but certainly well behind the halfway mark. Somehow it just seems a little safer there when you're a stranger in an unknown church.

I looked around, as is my habit in this circumstance, to see if I recognized anyone, or if by smiling directly at those around me someone might make eye contact and I could say good morning and strike up a small conversation. No luck. A dry well. Here comes that invisibility feeling again. Oh well, Hallelujah, He is risen!

Finally, as if by some mysterious signal, people began to cease their chatter and sit down in their pew and direct their attention toward the front

where someone official got the ball rolling.
Congregational hymns were sung, the choir
performed, prayers were prayed, offerings were
taken, and never had I felt an Easter Sunday to be
more perfunctory. Then came the sermon on this
most majestic of topics – the resurrection of Jesus
Christ from the dead – offered in a know-it-all style
of staccato phrases…kind of like the rat-tat-tat of a
machine gun, but filled with blanks. "Well," I said to
myself, "put down your self-righteousness, and back
away from your judgments. You don't know what is
going on in the hearts of these people, so just focus
on Jesus, give Him your attention, and get over
yourself." Good advice I might add, and I did my
best to take it. But my experience for the rest of
that Easter morning service was nevertheless
disfigured by the pervasive lack of hospitality. Not
one person looked our way, smiled at us, said hello,
or in any way acknowledged our presence. There
was a cold emptiness, a chilly indifference, a self-
centered preoccupation that left me, my wife, and
my grandson feeling unnoticed, disregarded, and
passed over. And we suffered this indifference at the
hands of the very people on whom God has
showered his love, grace, attention, help, presence,
inclusion – as the Apostle Paul said, "…who has
blessed us with every spiritual blessing in the
heavenly realms in Christ." (Ephesians 1.3) These
are the people who say "Jesus loves you," but act like

you don't exist when you visit their place of worship. They are the ones who advocate the idea that God has reached out in love to all of lost humanity through Jesus, but have little understanding of their own vitally important role in demonstrating that passionate interest in, and inclusiveness toward others. And the experience of this inhospitable spirit demonstrated not just by an individual, but by a whole community, amplified exponentially the dissonance between the theory of God's love and its reality lived out.

Because I am a believing Christian, what this experience produced in me was a deep grief. After church the three of us went to lunch at a nearby restaurant and I sat there quietly weeping because of what I saw in the life of this large and prosperous church. I wept for Jesus because of how poorly he was represented by these people for whom he died. And I wept for the people because of the dreadful deficiency of life that should enliven their interaction with each other, and especially with strangers. And I wept most bitterly for those people who are not believers who will visit this church and find demonstrated there something so foreign to the heart of God, and so off-putting that no matter how articulate the sermon, the message will be muddled and fall on deaf ears.

The hospitable church is powerful, but so is the inhospitable church. I hope this experience helps you see how important it is, for the sake of the Gospel, to move toward the former and away from the latter. But, there is another species of inhospitableness that I want to point out to you.

It was about six months later that my wife and I had another occasion to visit a church we had never been to before. We were in the Seattle area again seeing the kids and grandkids, and had heard about this church from friends in Santa Rosa. It is actually a kind of sister church, and so we were looking forward to seeing what it was like. And though our expectations were not too high, we did anticipate a positive and friendly experience.

Again, we didn't know what to expect. Would it be a small church or a large one? Would it be in a drab and dilapidated building, or something neat but uninteresting, or would it be welcoming and beautiful? I have strong feelings about things like architecture and how we Christians ought to care about such things, so was glad to find that the building itself was sensitively and thoughtfully put together. It was also a much larger building and congregation than our church at home which, for some reason, surprised me although it was a pleasant surprise.

We found a parking spot not too far from the front door, took a deep breath, and marched in. The ubiquitous greeters, armed with their usual stack of bulletins stood at the front door. There was a young-ish man on one side, and a young-ish woman on the other. Both were probably in their mid-20's, and were very much engaged in animated conversation with friends. As we walked in and waited in order to procure a bulletin, it became obvious that the conversation between greeters and friends was a much higher priority. No eye contact, no smile, no acknowledgement of our presence. It made me feel a bit awkward as we failed to secure a bulletin, but we proceeded on in and wended our way through a very animated and bustling crowd. We went into the sanctuary and spied out a couple of seats…again a bit more than half way back. We remained standing, (along with most of the people), and I again did my usual perusal of the throng, looking for anyone familiar or for a friendly face to engage in conversation. Again, no such luck. Again, here comes that invisible feeling.

There were many folks in this church locked in friendly conversation. There were smiles, handshakes, and hugs. There was loud laughter and obviously good friends catching up on each other's lives. That part was very good and I appreciated it. It was clear that here is a congregation which cares about relationships and loves one another. Awesome! Moreover, the worship music was beautiful and very skillfully led. The announcements were thoughtful and well-articulated. The sermon was inspiring and interesting.

After church, people again were quite involved in conversation and relationship. But not a soul greeted us or interacted with us in any way. No "Good morning" or "You look new, have I ever met you before?" or "My name's Paul, where are you from?"

Now you might think that compared to my Easter experience, this one was not nearly as bad. But, counter-intuitively, it was worse in some ways. And the reason for this is that the warm interaction between friends made me feel my status as stranger more intensely. I felt on the outside looking in. I felt more ignored because so many around me were not ignored. So the contrast between those on the inside and me on the outside was set in sharper relief for me.

So am I saying that it is not good for a church to be filled with people who are close friends, and can't wait to see each other on Sunday, and love to interact and be involved in each other's lives? No, a thousand times no! This is what the church should be, what God intended it to be, and what is made

197

possible because of the reconciling work of Jesus on the cross. This is the kind of church I want to be a part of – to be included in – and fortunately is the kind of church my wife and I have found here in our city. *But*, this is the kind of church whose strength is also its weakness in terms of hospitality, and needs very thoughtful and disciplined leadership to transform that weakness into additional strength.

Close friendships, loving relationships, rich fellowship; these are the very things that hospitality seeks to produce and experience. So the church in which these things are happening is already practicing hospitality in a very real sense. But by their very nature, close friendships tend to exclude the outsider. Being a good friend to someone else demands focused attention on that person. Have you ever had the experience where someone asks how you're doing, and you begin to answer in a less than superficial way, and then you notice the person you're talking to is looking around the room at other people rather than you? That trumpets very loudly that the person who asked "How are you?" was not really interested in an honest answer, and not really interested in you. Real hospitality calls for real focus when you're having a conversation. The people who are best at this make you feel like you're the only person in the room when you're in conversation with them.

So this creates a problem for churches that want to be hospitable. It is not easy to be true to the dual calling to "love one another," and to "make disciples of all the nations." It is not easy to be hospitable both inwardly and outwardly. It is difficult, in a tight circle of friends, for that circle to remain porous and generously include strangers. Selfishly, we often jealously guard that tight circle because someone new might change the dynamic in an unwelcome way.

This dual focus is difficult, yes, but it is absolutely necessary if we are to remain faithful to God's hospitable heart. So how, as churches, do we begin to remedy this thorny problem? Well, let me offer a few ideas for you to consider.

First, prayerfully start with yourself. You may or may not be a church leader or a pastor, but that's not the most important thing. The most important thing is to remember the ground we've already covered. Be hospitable to yourself by believing and receiving God's hospitality toward you. Feast at God's table so that you're filled with God's out-going love.

Second, prayerfully reach out hospitably toward others in your church. If you're in a church where this is already happening you are miles ahead. But if not, start with one person, be faithful, and believe the Kingdom principle that the yeast of your hospitality will work its way into the whole lump of dough. (Luke 13.20-21) Mother Theresa illustrated this Kingdom principle wonderfully when she was asked how her life had such a far-reaching influence, not only in the nation of India, but around the whole world. Her answer was that she always focused on *one*; she gave her attention to the *one* person who God had brought across her path. She was never overwhelmed by the huge numbers in poverty, and the thousands and millions without enough food or dying from sickness and disease. For her, the Kingdom of God always came down to one person, so she was satisfied to simply serve the one person in front of her at the moment. In so doing, she was able to change the whole world in the life of one person at a time, and it had a leavening effect that spread through the lives of tens of thousands of people. So be encouraged by Mother Theresa's example, and be faithful to serve one person at a time for God's Kingdom. In some mysterious way God will multiply the effect like yeast spreading through a lump of dough.

Third, prayerfully talk with the leaders of your church about hospitality. This will be particularly effective if you bring some ideas with you, and are willing to shoulder some responsibility.

Fourth, prayerfully consider some of the following

ideas as ones that might help your church move forward in hospitality.

- Gather a group of friends to read and discuss the ideas in this book, and keep track of any insights, and especially specific actions that you might take about how to live more hospitably.

- Think about creating a hospitality team – a group of people who would like to join you in growing as a hospitable person and a hospitable church.

Coffee and donuts after church is a great idea, but a wasted effort in terms of hospitality when it is just groups of the same old friends chatting together. To make hospitality successful in a church takes some *effort, thought, work, and faith.* What about training a team of people whose entire ministry on Sunday is to come alongside visitors or strangers, make them feel welcome, stick with them after church and have a conversation, ask them to lunch or over to dinner, or to come back next week and plan on going out to lunch then? Some visitors won't feel comfortable enough to say yes, but they will feel cared about – included – welcomed. Or maybe the goal of the ministry team could be to transform the "coffee and donuts" time after church into a process that would intentionally become more focused on deepening fellowship, giving attention to those who tend to be shy and including them in conversation, and particularly making sure that any visitor is genuinely welcomed and made to feel at home.

This team could include people who are already engaged in hospitality-oriented ministry. How about those "greeters", and the ushers, and other folks who help things run smoothly at church? They are actually very important in setting the tone – not only for new people who might be visiting, but also for the whole congregation. So meet together regularly (at least quarterly) with your hospitality team to pray, and communicate how to improve what you're doing, and to inspire each other.

It is important, among these people, to identify those who are particularly gifted in hospitality – those who are welcoming and inclusive – and hold them up as examples to learn from. But even though they may be gifted, they will still need equipping. This part can't be skipped. Greeters and others need to be given a vision for what they're doing. They need to understand that they have a strategic part in communicating the loving heart of God to anyone who darkens the door of your church. So if you're a greeter, for example, even though you may have good friends you want to talk to, you can't do it while you're greeting. Your first priority is to welcome everyone who is coming to church, and *especially* new people. Later on you can hang out with your buddies and talk with them.

To illustrate this let me tell you about Herb the greeter. Becky and I attended a Presbyterian church for a time, and the very first day we showed up we were greeted by a jovial and out-going man in his middle 70's. He smiled at us, asked us our names, handed us a bulletin, and engaged us in conversation. He made it clear he was delighted we were visiting his church, and also wanted to make sure we knew all the pertinent details. So he took us by the hand, walked us inside and showed us where the sanctuary was, where the fellowship hall was (where he promised to meet us after church so he could buy us a donut) and "most importantly," he said, "where the bathrooms are." Then he reiterated that he would track us down after the service and would take us to the fellowship hall for coffee and donuts. He was true to his word, waving and smiling to us over a sea of people, grabbing hold of us and pointing us in the right direction. Once there he supplied us with the promised refreshments, asked us more about our lives, introduced us to six or eight people, and made us feel completely welcome and at home in this large church to which we were total strangers. Needless to say, we returned the next

Sunday, and were just as enthusiastically greeted by Herb again, who was genuinely thrilled that we had come back a second week in a row. It was not only delightful to be the object of Herb's ministrations, but quite an eye-opener. I have never had such a welcoming experience walking in the front door of a church for the first time, and appreciated the rare privilege it was. But I also wondered to myself why it should be so rare. After all, the church is the object of God's grace, mercy, and redeeming love. Jesus gave his life for us, and welcomes us into intimate fellowship with him, irrespective of our checkered pasts, our brokennesses, and our sins. He walks with us moment by moment, fills us with his Holy Spirit, guards us with his superintending care, instructs us with his Word, and transforms us by his power. So this hospitality should be oozing from every pore. The church should be filled with Herbs!

So, if you are one of those "lowly greeters" in the church, let the grace of God and the example of Herb inspire you. You have an awesome responsibility and a rare privilege to express in real terms the reality of the Kingdom of God to people who may have never heard about it, or haven't experienced its welcome for many years. If you're "just an average lay-person," let the people and stories and ideas in this book help you see that you are far more than that. You are "a chosen people, a royal priesthood, a holy nation, a people belonging to God, that you may declare the praises of Him who called you out of darkness into His wonderful light." (1Peter2.9) As a royal priest of the one true God, you have the opportunity, through hospitality, to demonstrate the marvel of who this wonderful God is. At church on Sunday morning you can look around, see who's new or lonely, and become a welcomer. You don't need a degree from seminary, or papers of ordination, or the official imprimatur of the board of elders or deacons. If you are a believer, God has already made you a royal priest. So you already have the responsibility and authority to pass along his hospitable welcome to all those who cross your path, whether in church or in the marketplace.

- Organize a rainy day crew.

Why not recruit a bunch of young guys and girls to be the rainy day crew? This is especially great if you live in a place like Seattle where it seems to rain about 75% of the time. Ask people in your church to donate a bunch of umbrellas, and have the crew prepared on rainy days to wait at a strategic place where they can run out to cars that are driving up and provide umbrella coverage to folks as they go from parking lot to church building. It is an extremely hospitable and thoughtful thing to do, and will be a blessing to visitors and veterans alike. This is just one idea of hundreds that might take shape as you think about hospitality.

- Become a stranger. Go by yourself, or with not more than one friend, to a church you've never attended before.

Be very observant of your own feelings and reactions to the way you are treated. Learn from both the good things and the bad. Particularly think about how you could include the good experiences in your own church, and how you would want to be treated differently in terms of the bad things. Then honestly think about how you might be making some of the same mistakes in your church, and how they could be addressed. Meet with your hospitality team and talk about what you saw and felt and brainstorm about things you might do.

- Energize giftedness. Identify those in your church who are particularly gifted in hospitality, and ask them to disciple others in their giftedness.

Very simply, if you are interested in hospitality, hang out with those who have hospitality gifts. In that context, you can soak up their giftedness, their love of people, their excitement about opening their home to the lonely and those in need of healing. Let them impart to you their wisdom and skill and generosity of heart. Be their apprentice in learning how to make others feel welcome and valuable. Let them be hospitable to you so you can feel how it feels, and then you can go and do the same for others. Have them involve you in the process of putting on a dinner (or better yet, several dinners over a period of six months) which would include a stranger or two as well as friends. Each time, talk about principles of hospitality; what you learned, what worked and didn't work, how to do better, etc. Pray together that God would bless your efforts and use your hospitality to bring hope, healing, encouragement and a sense of at-home-ness to those you've invited. Also, *and this is important*, talk with those involved in this process about how to bring that same sense of inclusion into your church gatherings. Maybe even work on training members of the congregation to be especially aware of visitors or people they have never met before, and give them practical help in how to have a conversation with a complete stranger.

If you're married, do this together as a couple. If you're single, find a friend or recruit a roommate or two, and learn this kingdom calling as a team. Hospitality, like most ministry, usually works better with teamwork. You can pray together, divide responsibilities, be a catalyst for each other's creativity, and rejoice together as you see God work through you.

> • Leave room for hospitality. Especially on Sundays, come to church with the expectation that you're going to invite someone home for a meal, or out to lunch or coffee.

Looking at the second example I gave of the inhospitable church, what a huge difference it would have made to me and my wife if someone had struck up a conversation with us and invited us to coffee afterward. We may or may not have accepted the invitation, depending on many variables, but we would have felt noticed, cared about and included. We would have experienced, more fully, God's personal interest in us, if a person in the church had shown any interest in us.

If you have a lot of friends at church that you look forward to catching up with each Sunday – that is a very good thing. But don't forget that making room for hospitality requires that you make room for strangers. Make it your goal to talk to at least one person each Sunday who you have never met, or at least who you barely know. Be curious about them. Find out their name, where they're from, what they do for a living, what they're interested in outside of work, if they have children, what or who brought them to church, if they go to church regularly, etc. Tell them you're glad they came, and would love it if they came again soon. Introduce them to somebody you know.

Imagine that you were a visitor to your church and nobody spoke to you or looked at you during the service or as you left. Maybe it was a well- managed church service. The worship was up-lifting and the musicians were practiced and talented. Perhaps the people who made announcements about various church activities were articulate and friendly in their demeanor and the sermon was well presented and thoughtful. But for me, I want church to be more than a well-produced show. I can get that on Sunday morning TV, and don't have to go to all the trouble to get up, drive to some particular place, sit in a questionably comfortable pew or chair, and deal with a crowd of people who totally ignore me.

Church needs to be, especially for the visitor or stranger, a place where the message preached is incarnated in its people. If the message is that God loves me, cares about my needs, and welcomes me into a relationship with him, but the people who communicate this message treat me like I'm unseen, or act as if I don't exist, then the message gets confused, befuddled, lost. God's people need to shut up about love until they can learn to act hospitably toward one another, and especially toward strangers and visitors. Talk is cheap. Actions speak louder than words. I know it is easier, and more fun and comfortable, to spend time chatting and catching up with your friends at church on Sunday morning, or whenever your church meets. But if there are strangers who have screwed up their courage and risked coming into your church building to hear about your God, RED ALERT! DROP EVERYTHING! Notice the visitor, acknowledge the presence of the stranger, make eye contact with the sojourner, welcome the seeker, engage the alien in conversation, act like he matters. Then, when he hears the sermon perhaps he will make a connection between the theory taught, and the life lived by the people who ascribe to that theory. Maybe when he hears about a God who loves him, and then meets people who act lovingly toward him, the two will come together in a powerful way to convince him that it's true. Maybe he or she will experience the healing hand of God because you were hospitable to them.

VISUALIZE THE IDEAL

Have you ever had an experience of hospitality, whether in church or in some other venue, that left an impression on you and made you hungry for more? Make use of that experience to help you imagine what it might be like to be part of a truly hospitable church. Let me give you an example from my own experience.

My wife and I, before we were married and were still in college, visited a church together in Los Angeles. We had heard about this church as one that was particularly interesting and dynamic, and we wanted to see what it was like. We hadn't heard a lot of details so our expectations were somewhat vague, but the experience turned out to be amazingly powerful. The pastor at this church was extremely engaging as a preacher, and had some interesting and challenging things to say. The worship was vibrant and uplifting and we appreciated it deeply. But all of that paled in significance compared to the hospitality that was demonstrated by the people of this church.

As the service ended and we were thinking about leaving, someone nearby introduced himself to us and began asking us about who we were. We told them we had driven down from Santa Barbara, that we were students at Westmont College, etc. He asked what we were studying; we inquired about his life and what he thought about the church. He introduced us to several people around us, and they all participated with us in conversation – eager to know who we were and what we were up to. This same group of people then prevailed upon us to join them for dinner at the home of the man who originally greeted us. Curious, and eager to find out what made these people tick, we gladly accepted. We walked just a block or so to the home of our host, and there we were included, as if old friends, in a fascinating and animated conversation around a delicious meal. We talked about the content of the sermon, about the Christian life, about various experiences in learning how to walk with Jesus; we laughed uproariously, prayed together earnestly, and were treated like the angels that Scripture says we might have been. (Although I assure you we were not!) But when all was said and done, we were deeply affected by one of the most remarkable experiences of hospitality we had ever had. It made a lasting impression, and had we lived in Los Angeles we would have come again, and been interested in discovering more of what this church was all about.

Now think together with me about this experience. Here was a group of people whom we had never met, but who eagerly welcomed us into their very tight circle of fellowship. Their welcome said to us "You belong here; we're glad to include you as one of us." None of them knew we were coming to visit their church, yet on the spur of the moment they were enthusiastically willing to drop everything to make a couple of college strangers feel at home.

When our host said "Why don't we all go to my house for dinner?" no calendars needed to be consulted, no regrets were expressed. Everyone simply said "Sure, let's go." I imagine these were people who had determined ahead of time that hospitality was a priority. I also imagine that they tended to be prepared for this kind of experience. They loved each other, so they loved to hang out together after church. I wouldn't be surprised if, embedded in their idea of "church," was the notion that the worship service wasn't over when the benediction was given. It was probably assumed that there would be lots of fellowshipping in each other's homes after church, and anyone who might be visiting would gladly be included. To me, this was a church that, by their expression of hospitality, deeply experienced the reality of community, and had made the vital connection between receiving God's hospitable welcome in their own lives, and sharing that welcome with others.

This is important stuff. The way we communicate the character of God is at stake here. And the mission of the church to be a change agent for good within a culture is at stake here. The sincerity of the prayer that many of us pray regularly, "Thy Kingdom come; Thy will be done on earth as it is in heaven," is at stake here. That prayer is nothing but vain repetition, and our mission in the world is nothing but a vapid platitude – unless and until we open our hearts in hospitality.

I know for many individuals, and for many churches, this calls for a major paradigm shift. It cuts across the grain of our self-indulgence and challenges our comfortable complacency. It demands a realignment of our values and of how we invest our time and energy. But in the West, our culture is crumbling for want of the salt and light of the Gospel lived authentically through God's people. And from my perspective, hospitality is at the heart of what is wanting.

If you've read this far, you must be someone who cares about these things – whose heart is moved by the need around us for folks to find a place to call home among a hospitable people who are committed to God's purposes in the world. And if you are one of those people, my hope is that you will take to heart some of the suggestions and stories and exhortations you've been reading. Ruminate in the hospitality of God toward you, and then share it with others. Talk to some friends at church and form a hospitality ministry team. Call some people you'd like to know better and have them to dinner. Create some space after church on Sundays to share coffee, or lunch, or a walk in the park with friends and strangers.

These are relatively small things really – not great sacrifices – but they are actions made significant by their potential to change the world in the life of one person. When the deep wound of the loss of home in a person's life is touched by the welcoming embrace of Jesus' people, then the bumper stickers we read might begin to change from "Jesus, save me from your people," to "Jesus, I've found a home among your people."

INVITED HOME

XIII. FINDING HOME

Since the fall of Adam and Eve in the Garden of Eden, man has been homeless in the universe, and this loss of home is one way to describe our deepest wound. We all know something of the sense of alienation and homelessness that life presents us with. Most of us have had experiences of loneliness and isolation – whether it was being bullied in school, or picked last for the baseball team at recess, or failing a test, or being rejected by a girlfriend or boyfriend, or being wrongly accused by people you thought were friends, or being fired from a job and wondering how you'd make ends meet, and if anyone cared. Whether it is anxiety and depression, or fear of failure, or our obsessive need to be accepted by or pleasing to others; whether it is anger or hatred or sadness or insecurity – and all the behaviors that arise from these pathologies – our frantic efforts and our quiet desperation can usually be traced back to our primal need to find the home we have lost. Without a home, it is not a given that we have the right to exist, and without the right to exist we have no value and no meaning or purpose to our lives. This is the human dilemma and it is all connected to the basic wound of homelessness. The result is that we are now on the outside looking in, as it were; wandering from place to place trying to find the one place that fits who we are – that makes us feel at home – that provides a sense of security, and satisfaction, and comfort, and belonging.

The stories and ideas we have looked at in the previous chapters have attempted to address this situation we find ourselves in. The big idea I have advanced is that homelessness and hospitality are like mirror images in a sense; one is the problem, and the other is the solution. I have shared stories from the Bible and from my life which suggest that although human hospitality is a wonderful salve for our woundedness, the ultimate healing for homelessness is to experience the hospitable heart of God. Accordingly, it has been my heart's desire to help you see God's character in this way. As a pastor it has been my experience that even people who have believed in God for years and years often do not see him as the gracious and merciful and hospitable God he actually is. So based on the presupposition that the Bible is God's revelation of himself, we have looked at many examples in the Bible that powerfully demonstrate his hospitable heart – his open arms and his welcoming invitation to anyone who is interested in a relationship with him.

Now, in this final chapter, I'd like to do what I promised, and explain for anyone who may not know, or who may have never heard, that there really is a way to experience a relationship with this hospitable and gracious God. The very good news is that being at home with God, and your experience of his hospitality, is a gift freely offered. Further, it need not be a vague and illusive thing – but something about which you can be certain, and which will give your life that foundation of granite which I described in an earlier chapter.

In order to explain this let's return once more to the Bible, and re-visit the story of the Prodigal Son and the Prodigious Father, because this story contains – in capsulized form – the Story of Stories. It guides us into the discovery of what God has done for us through Jesus – and it is that story that we need to not just hear, but enter into – in order to find our way home.

You'll remember at the beginning of the parable that the younger of two sons went to his father and asked for his share of the estate. (Luke 16.11ff.) Perhaps he felt that life at home was too restrictive and demanding. He probably wanted to go out on his own and experience "true freedom," breaking loose from the moral strictures he had been taught growing up. It's likely he reasoned that he needed to find an environment where he felt "accepted for who he was," and in which he could indulge all his lusts and desires. We know from his subsequent actions that this was clearly his purpose, and he went at it with a vengeance, "...squander[ing] his wealth in wild living." (v.13). But reality finally brought him up short. After he had spent all his money he discovered that what he thought was freedom had actually led him into a worse bondage than the one he felt at home. The people who were his close buddies when he had money were now strangely absent. The women who loved him were now aloof. The welcome into clubs and social circles which his money had purchased for him was now withdrawn. He began to see the harsh reality that the belonging he felt among his new and adventurous friends was only as deep as his pockets. As quickly as his newfound wealth came, it was gone, and in its place grew hunger, loneliness, and probably a sense of shame. He found himself, like us, on the outside looking in, and longing for a home where he was truly welcome, without condition.

Now this is the first point where we have to be cautious in reading this parable. Many people can identify with this young man, and if you're one of those folks, then so far you're doing fine in "getting" the story. But there are many others who think "Well, I may have done a few bad things in my life, but at least I'm not as foolish as this guy…in fact I'm really a basically good person, and I don't identify with this story at all." In that case, Jesus has you trapped, because you then fit into the category of the older sibling, the one I call the "Pugnacious Brother." In both cases, the need was exactly the same. Although one brother was hyper-decadent and the other brother was hyper-responsible, both had the same problem. Both misunderstood what it meant to be a son, and thus neither was really "at home" with their father. Even though one had gone away to a far country, and the other had stayed dutifully at home, both were really on the outside looking in. Both needed to find home. What this parable explains to us about ourselves is that all of us are in the same boat in relationship to our Heavenly Father. Religious or rebellious, naughty or nice, prodigal or pugnacious – as the Apostle Paul said in (Romans 3.23); "…for *all* have sinned and fall short of the glory of God." (Italics mine.)

But let's return to the younger son in his hungry and desperate situation. Once all his money was gone he hired himself out to a farmer to feed his pigs, and was so hungry he actually wanted to eat the food he was giving the pigs, "…but no one gave him anything." (v.16.) This is a key point in the story, because it conveys that the younger brother finally "got it." It says that he "…came to his senses." (v.17) Wow; an epiphany; an aha moment. He had to leave home to discover that there really was a home that had been there all along for him to enjoy. There really was a place where he had belonged – a place in his father's house where he was wanted, and valued, and could contribute. He realized that in his foolishness he had squandered all of that, but now he hoped against hope that if he groveled and ate enough crow, perhaps his father would accept him back – certainly not as a son, but maybe as a hired hand – where at least he might have enough to eat, and a dry place to sleep.

Again, the parable skillfully reveals something very significant about us and our relationship with our Father in heaven. Whether you know that such a home has always existed – that it has always been there for you to enjoy; or whether you have been the kind of person who, like me, had never heard about such a place, I think we have been able to identify the fact that we all long for it. Yet, like the prodigal son, in some measure we have foolishly thought we could create a home for ourselves – on our own –

with no need for the home God has created for us. But usually in life, at some point our longing for home becomes so acute that most of us begin to wonder if there really is a spiritual home that we need to find – a place that will meet the deepest longings of our heart. That is the point at which, like the prodigal son, we "come to our senses." And often, like him, we reason that perhaps if we grovel enough, work enough, be good enough or religious enough, try hard enough, or perform well enough, we might earn our way back home, at least as a servant or hired hand.

But now we come to the heart of the story, because we come in contact with the heart of God through the surprising, and altogether unearned and undeserved reaction of the Prodigious Father.

Imagine yourself in the place of the prodigal son; weak, weary, emaciated, scraggly, sick – dragging yourself along the dusty road that leads to home. You've rehearsed your self-deprecating speech, but your stomach is in a knot, dreading the reaction of the father whose heart, and life, and values you so thoroughly rejected. Several times along the way you turned around, but you realized you had nowhere else to go so you reluctantly went forward, but the closer you got to home, the more intense your feelings of shame became. And then at last, nearly in view of your old home, you see a cloud of dust arising from the middle of the road, and out of the midst of that cloud – at first just a speck, but soon big enough to recognize – the unmistakable silhouette of your father – running toward you as fast as his feet can carry him – arms waving crazily, and robes flapping in the wind. What's that in his hand; a club to beat you over the head, or just a figment of your imagination? As he gets close your head sags and your eyes can only fix themselves on the dirt at your feet – but you can tell by the rapid footfalls that he isn't slowing down. You cringe, awaiting scathing words and painful blows, when your expectations are suddenly and wonderfully un-met. His arms are thrown around you, his lips kiss your neck, and his hot tears mingle with yours.

Too good to be true, this unlooked for embrace produces in you an unimagined ecstasy that you can't quite allow yourself to feel. As you try to spit out your speech of repentance your father grabs your face in both hands, looks deeply into your eyes with a smile of joy and a laugh of dismissal – as if to say "There's no need. Welcome home son." And then shouting to his servants who had just arrived on the scene huffing and puffing in hot pursuit to see what was amiss, your father orders them to bring robe, ring, and sandals – the symbols of full sonship – followed by a great feast of celebration because things have been put right, and you're back where you belong.

Too good to be true, indeed, and yet this is the good news and the truth. This parable of the prodigal is one among many from the Bible that reveals the hospitable heart of God. Through it, Jesus is inviting us to come home to our Father – to find that place of welcome and belonging that was lost to us in Eden. And he made it very clear that the invitation is a gift that cannot be earned or deserved. The only condition is that we come to our senses; that we leave that far country of rebellion and self-assertion and self-absorption, and accept God's invitation to come home.

"But wait a minute," I can imagine some of you saying. "This is all very nice, but what about the issue of right and wrong? Are you saying to me that God doesn't really care about any of the things the prodigal did? Has he changed his mind about the Law and no longer requires a person to be righteous in order to have a relationship with him? Is the New Testament just a giant u-turn by God in which he is declaring that he has changed his mind about morality and goodness, and he has now simply decided to overlook it and relax about such archaic issues?"

If you wondered about this, then you asked a very

good and very important question – and one not really addressed by the parable itself. It is an important part of the Story of Stories, and something we need to look at in order to understand the full story.

At first it might appear that the parable of the prodigal son is saying just that; that God has changed his mind about right and wrong, and that he no longer has a problem with evil. But if that were true then God would no longer be good, would he, since true goodness hates evil. So the real question is how can God forgive the evil we do, as Jesus asserts in the parable, and still remain holy, righteous, and good? Remember, the New Testament says that all have sinned and fall short of the glory of God (Rom.3.23), and that the penalty for that sin is death. (Rom.6.23)

It is in the midst of this dilemma that we see the true grace, mercy and hospitality of God. In his goodness the penalty must be paid, but in his love and hospitable desire to restore us to our true home, he chose to pay the penalty for us by dying in our place as our substitute.

Substitute!!?? What do I mean by substitute? Well, the Old Testament has dozens, if not hundreds of examples of "substitution" – and each of these examples is God's way of pointing to, and explaining what Jesus would eventually do for us on the cross. Let me take you to one more story from the Bible – one of my favorites – as an example of what I mean. It is another father / son story, but in this case not a parable, but the reporting of historical fact.

1 After these things God tested Abraham and said to him, "Abraham!" "Here I am," he answered. **2** "Take your son," He said, "your only [son] Isaac, whom you love, go to the land of Moriah, and offer him there as a burnt offering on one of the mountains I will tell you about." **3** So Abraham got up early in the morning, saddled his donkey, and took with him two of his young men and his son Isaac. He split wood for a burnt offering and set out to go to the place God had told him about. **4** On the third day Abraham looked up and saw the place in the distance. **5** Then Abraham said to his young men, "Stay here with the donkey. The boy and I will go over there to worship; then we'll come back to you." **6** Abraham took the wood for the burnt offering and laid it on his son Isaac. In his hand he took the fire and the sacrificial knife, and the two of them walked on together. **7** Then Isaac spoke to his father Abraham and said, "My father." And he replied, "Here I am, my son." Isaac said, "The fire and the wood are here, but where is the lamb for the burnt offering?" **8** Abraham answered, "God Himself will provide the lamb for the burnt offering, my son." Then the two of them walked on together. **9** When they arrived at the place that God had told him about, Abraham built the altar there and arranged the wood. He bound his son Isaac and placed him on the altar on top of the wood. **10** Then Abraham reached out and took the knife to slaughter his son. **11** But the Angel of the LORD called to him from heaven and said, "Abraham, Abraham!" He replied, "Here I am." **12** Then He said, "Do not lay a hand on the boy or do anything to him. For now I know that you fear God, since you have not withheld your only son from Me."

13 Abraham looked up and saw a ram caught in the thicket by its horns. So Abraham went and took the ram and offered it as a burnt offering in place of his son. **14** And Abraham named that place The LORD Will Provide, so today it is said: "It will be provided on the LORD's mountain." (Gen 22:1-14 - HCSB)

God had many purposes for this interaction with Abraham around the sacrifice of his son Isaac, but clearly one of those purposes was to foreshadow what he would do through Jesus. In (v.8) we see that Abraham believed God would provide a *substitute* to take Isaac's place as a sacrifice. And (v.13) shows that Abraham's faith was vindicated. "Abraham looked up and saw a ram caught in the thicket by its horns. So Abraham went and took the ram and offered it as a burnt offering *in place of* his son."

In the parable of the Prodigal Son and the Prodigious Father Jesus doesn't explain the part about the substitute, but maybe that's because the Substitute Himself was the one giving the parable. The people he told the parable to, likely had the same question about forgiveness – and it was probably by design. Jesus was revealing the heart of the Father, while at the same time drawing peoples' gaze toward him as the solution to the un-answered question of forgiveness. Jesus knew that his death on a cross would make this forgiveness possible. He died in our place, as our substitute, taking on himself the punishment and penalty for our sin, so that God would be free to be the prodigious father of the parable. In Jesus, God's demand for a payment for sin is fully satisfied, so he is completely free to welcome us home – safe and secure in his kiss and embrace – not a second-class citizen but a full son with robe, ring, and sandals – and celebrated over by a father whose heart has ached and longed for us to return to him.

If this is true, what's the catch? What do I have to do to earn this standing with God? Well, again, look at the parable. You can see that the son thought a groveling speech of mea culpa might earn him a place on the outskirts of his father's acceptance - perhaps as a hired servant. This is really what religion is all about. It's the idea that if I do enough right things, maybe they will eventually out-weigh the wrong things, and thus will earn my way back into God's favor. If I can be humble enough, contrite enough, ashamed enough – then maybe God will have compassion on me and allow me at least into the fringes of heaven. But Jesus exploded that idea totally in this wonderful parable. The father was completely un-interested in blame and shame. He wanted nothing of his son's efforts to earn his way back into his good graces. His open heart of hospitable welcome was a free and un-earnable gift that he longed to give to his son. It was simply a matter of the son's decision to leave his foolishness, return to his father, and receive the gift freely offered to him.

So there you have it! If you are looking in from the outside, and "finding home" is something you long for – I hope you can see that there is nothing in the heart of God that would keep you in your homeless condition. His gift of hospitality is eagerly offered to anyone who – like dear Zacchaeus in chapter IV – is willing to receive the invitation of Jesus to dine with him.

If you're still out there wandering, I encourage you – come to your senses. Come home. The hospitable heart of God beats for you – as he longs to hug you, kiss your neck, include you in full sonship, and celebrate your homecoming.

If that's your desire, then listen to these ancient words of the Apostle John; "…To all who received him, to those who believed in his name, he gave the right to become children of God…" (John.1.12) This passage explains that you will receive the Father's open welcome by believing in Jesus. To believe in him means to simply open the empty hands of faith, choosing to trust that Jesus' work on the cross was and is the all-sufficient and only requirement to come into a relationship with God your true father. If you're ready, simply talk to him. Tell him you want to come home, and you believe in what Jesus did on the cross to make that possible. Jesus said in (Revelation 3.20) that if you open your heart to him in that way, your experience of his hospitality will begin, because he will come into your life and dine with you. In him you will find your true home. You're invited, and it's my heart's desire, and certainly his, that you will decide to receive God's "Welcome home" today.

INVITED HOME

APPENDIX: HELPFUL HINTS AND RECIPES

This appendix is designed to address the two basic kinds of convivia that I addressed – the last-minute/informal/spontaneous type, as well as the more carefully planned-ahead variety. The first part are examples of menus and supplies that will make your "lunches with Greg and Jacob" more possible and less vulnerable to the excuses that keep our lives shallow and disengaged from the adventure of hospitality that God invites us into. These are meals that can come together solely from things you've already got in your pantry, or freezer, or that you can pick up on a quick trip to the grocery store.

---

1. *Pasta al Café Citti.*

Café Citti is a charming, rustic Italian bistro located in the little village of Kenwood, just a few miles from where we live. The food there is simple and delicious, and relatively inexpensive - just the place to go on a warm summer's night and dine on the tiny patio under the bright stars and enormous oak tree. They have a dozen or so pasta dishes, delicious chicken, and the most garlicky Caesar salad you'll ever get a whiff of. My favorite thing to eat there is the linguine with pancetta, garlic, red pepper flakes and olive oil. It is so simple that I was able to copy it without having to ask for a recipe. I have made it many times for guests, who tend to rave about it. It is quick and easy and I hope you'll try it and like it as much as I do.

- 1 lb. linguine (or spaghetti, or fettuccini - whatever you prefer, or happen to have on hand.)
- ¼ lb. pancetta thickly sliced and chopped into a small dice. (Use bacon if you don't have pancetta - it's almost as good.)
- 1 whole head of garlic, each clove separated, peeled, and chopped into a large dice. (Each clove, depending on its size, gets chopped into about 4-6 pieces)
- ¼ cup shredded parmesan cheese (give or take, depending on your taste.)
- Pinch of red pepper flakes
- 1/3 cup olive oil.

Fill a large (6-8 qt.) pot with water and bring to a boil over high heat.

While you're waiting for the water to boil cut up the pancetta and the garlic cloves. (This part takes a little time, but I usually have guests sit at the counter and talk with me while I'm cooking, so they're not sitting alone in the living room strumming their fingers and waiting for dinner.) Heat a large skillet (at least 12 inches) over medium high heat and add 2 Tablespoons olive oil. When the oil is hot add the pancetta and saute until it is about half done and most of the fat is rendered. (approx 5 minutes.) Add the garlic and a pinch or two of red pepper flakes (depending on your heat preference). Sauté for another 5 minutes or so, being careful to not burn the garlic which makes it bitter. You want the garlic to become golden brown, but not dark brown, so keep an eye on it. When it's done reduce the heat to low and keep it warm.

Meanwhile, sometime in the middle of this process your water has come to a boil. Add a generous 2 tablespoons of salt to the water - this is important! - and a good glug of olive oil. Then add the pasta and stir carefully so it doesn't stick to itself. After it returns to a boil let it cook for 8-10 minutes so its soft but not squishy.

When the garlic and pancetta are done, and the pasta is ready, don't drain the pasta. Instead, with a pasta fork (or whatever tool works for you) scoop the pasta out of the pot and into the skillet with the garlic mixture, letting a little of the pasta water drip into the pan. Add the rest of the olive oil and a handful of the parmesan cheese and mix well. If it needs a little more sauce add a bit more pasta water. Season with salt and pepper and pour out onto a heated platter or large bowl. Serve extra parmesan alongside. You're gonna LOVE this.

With this meal I would serve a Caesar salad, (recipe following) a glass of wine, (you know, the stuff that Jesus turned water into), and if your guests are really hungry or there are lots of them, I might pick up an already-roasted chicken at the grocery store, cut it up, and serve it on another platter.

The Godfather's Caesar Salad

Francis Ford Coppola, the director of the famous Godfather trilogy, has a wonderful winery just a few minutes north of us near a town called Geyserville. At his winery there is a restaurant called Rustic where they serve a delicious Caesar salad. Becky and I like to go there and sit out on the terrace overlooking rolling hills and lush green vineyards. On a beautiful, warm, sunny afternoon or evening, we will order this Caesar salad and devour it eagerly while imagining ourselves in Tuscany. Because a Caesar salad is all about the dressing, we were able to coax the recipe for the dressing from our waiter who wrote it out in tiny letters on the back of our dinner check. Here's an approximation of what he wrote:

Dressing
- 2 teaspoons of anchovy paste
- 2 cloves of garlic finely minced
- 1 teaspoon of Dijon mustard. (I prefer the Maille brand, but Grey Poupon is fine.)
- 1 raw egg
- Juice of ½ lemon
- 2 tablespoons red wine vinegar
- 1 teaspoon Worcestershire sauce
- 1/3 cup olive oil
- Salt and pepper
- 2 tablespoons grated parmesan cheese.

Squish first three ingredients together thoroughly with the back of a fork until they are well married. Then add each remaining ingredient, one at a time, mixing well with whisk. Pour over romaine lettuce cut or torn into bite size pieces. Delicious with homemade croutons made with crusty Italian bread, cut into 1 inch cubes, and sautéed in butter till golden brown.

---

2. Tortilla Soup a la Helene w/ Cheesy Corn Bread

Our good friend Helene made this tortilla soup for dinner one evening, and we were hooked. It is absolutely delicious and incredibly simple. If you know how to open a can and chop a few vegetables, you're all set.

Combine and simmer over low heat for one hour:
- 2 16 oz. cans chopped tomatoes
- 2 8 oz. cans tomato sauce
- 2 cloves garlic, minced
- 4 cups water
- 2 tbsp. sugar
- 1 tbsp. chili powder
- 2 tsp. salt
- ½ tsp. pepper
- ½ tsp. oregano
- 1 4 oz. can chopped Ortega green chilies

Add 2 cups (or more) cooked shredded chicken at the last minute, simmering long enough just to heat through. NOTE: I like to buy an already roasted chicken and use all the meat – both light and dark. Some people prefer to only use the breast meat.

To serve put a handful of tortilla chips in a large soup bowl and ladle soup right over the chips. Top with (and this is really important) the following condiments:

- Sour cream
- Diced avocado
- Grated sharp cheddar and grated jack cheese
- Sliced black olives (from a can.)
- Chopped fresh tomatoes
- Chopped green onions

Now, this soup is really fantastic, but Helene served it accompanied by her cheesy corn bread, and if you don't try this you'll be very sorry! It takes a little time, so might not work for a VERY last minute meal, but if your guests are patient they will be well rewarded.

While soup is cooking, in a large bowl cream together

- 1 cup butter
- 1 cup sugar

Add 4 eggs and beat until smooth.
Stir in

- 1 16 oz. can creamed corn (really!)
- ½ cup grated jack cheese
- ½ cup grated sharp cheddar cheese

Sift together and stir in

- 1 cup flour
- 1 cup yellow corn meal
- 4 tsp. baking powder
- ½ tsp. salt

Pour into a 9" x 13" baking pan, and bake in a preheated 375 degree oven for 30-40 minutes, or until top is golden brown. My guests invariably say this is the best corn bread they have ever eaten. Delish!

---

3. *Sausage Pasta "Bon Marche"*

There used to be a department store in Seattle called the Bon Marche.   One day in their kitchen department where they sold Calphalon pots and pans Becky and I encountered a very sweet lady demonstrating how great the pans were. She had made a delicious pasta dish as part of her demonstration, and she gladly gave us the recipe. Our sons and their friends always loved it when I threw this together at the last minute, and it is still an easy-to-make favorite.

Cook 1 lb. of penne pasta (or whatever you prefer) according to package directions in a large pot of boiling salted water with a glug of olive oil. NOTE: Use at least a full tablespoon of salt in the water or the pasta will be bland.

While pasta is cooking, over medium high heat, in a large skillet, brown 1 lb. breakfast sausage links, cut into 1½" pieces, in 2 tbsp. olive oil.

Remove sausage from pan, and sauté in the pan drippings (adding more oil if necessary)
- ½ large onion, chopped
- 2 cloves garlic, minced

Return sausage to pan, and add
- 1 16 oz. can diced tomatoes with juice
- 1 8 oz. can tomato sauce
- 1 tbsp. tomato paste (Hint: If you get the kind that comes in a toothpaste-style tube you don't waste a whole can – you just squeeze out the amount you need and put the rest back in the fridge.)
- 1 tsp. sugar (this is an important trick to balance the acidity of the tomatoes.)
- Salt and pepper to taste
- Dash of oregano

- Dash of red pepper flakes (This is optional, but I like just a little to give the sauce a bit of a kick.)

Simmer to reduce until thickened – approximately 10 – 15 minutes.

Add ½ cup whipping cream and simmer 5 to 10 more minutes to blend flavors and thicken a bit more.

Drain pasta and add to sauce in skillet, mixing thoroughly so all the pasta is well coated.
Serve with grated parmesan cheese alongside so each person can add as much as they like. (I like a ton.)

---

4. The Complete Do-Almost-Nothing Dinner

This one is not a recipe, but just a menu – a way to put together a meal last minute when you absolutely have no time and nothing in the fridge or pantry.

- An already roasted chicken. (These are fairly ubiquitous nowadays in the grocery store, and have saved me many times when I needed something right now and didn't have the time to cook. They are usually delicious, inexpensive, and often come seasoned in a variety of ways.)

- A jar of already-made chicken gravy.
- A can of cranberry sauce.
- A box of stove-top stuffing.
- A bag of already-made Caesar salad, including croutons and dressing.
- Anything you like out of the baked-goods case of your grocery store for dessert.

Gently heat up the gravy in a small saucepan. While it is heating;

Make the stuffing according to package directions.
Put the cranberry sauce in a pretty serving dish.
Put the gravy into a small pitcher or gravy boat.
Put the stuffing into an appropriate serving bowl.
Cut up the chicken into 8 pieces (2 breasts, 2 thighs, 2 legs, 2 wings) and arrange attractively on a small platter.

Toss all the Caesar salad ingredients together in a salad bowl.

Put it all on the table and have each person serve himself "family-style."

When everyone is done, clear off the table and serve the dessert along with cups of coffee or tea.

NOTE: It is often appropriate, especially if it is a last-minute gathering, to ask each guest to bring one ingredient. They can stop by the grocery store on the way to your house. Most people understand that it is expensive to have guests to a meal, and are willing to contribute. It is easy on everyone if one guest brings the gravy, another the cranberry sauce, etc. If you've already got this menu in your head then you know exactly what to ask each person to bring – you're the initiator and organizer, but it's an easy, no-brainer, and you are creating community and hospitality. Fun and easy!

Here are my suggestions for three planned-ahead, not-quick meals. These are the specially premeditated, more sumptuous expressions of hospitality designed for celebrating with friends and strangers. They can be for the purpose of marking a special occasion, or just because you love, appreciate, and celebrate the people God has brought into your life. In this appendix I am sharing three ideas that Becky and I frequently use in one way or another.

This first one is an annual event for us. Every Fall we pull out our Jamaican Stuffed Pumpkin recipe and invite folks who might enjoy something a little different. Usually people eagerly come to this celebration out of curiosity – "What on earth is

Jamaican stuffed pumpkin?" We always wonder if people will really enjoy it, and they invariably do, so we continue the tradition.

A HARVEST DINNER (for 6-8 people)

Jamaican Stuffed Pumpkin

Cut a circular top out of one 8 – 10 inch sugar pumpkin. (Save for lid.) Scoop out seeds, and discard, and scrape inside clean of little strings. Place pumpkin in a large stock pot, and cover with salted water. Bring to a boil, simmer until the pumpkin is almost tender when pierced with a fork, about 10 minutes. Pumpkin should still be firm enough to hold its shape well. Watch carefully and check often.

Meat Stuffing – Preheat oven to 350.
- 2 Tbsp. salad oil
- 2 lb. lean ground beef
- 6 oz. ground smoked ham. (I buy a thick slice of ham at the grocery store and chop it up in the food processor.
- 2 ½ c. finely chopped onion

Combine and cook over medium high heat, stirring,

until meat is browned and crumbly. Remove from heat and pour off most of the fat.

Mix together:
- 1 ½ tsp. salt
- 2 tsp. olive oil
- 2 tsp. oregano
- 1 tsp. red wine vinegar
- 1 tsp. ground black pepper
- 1 tsp. minced garlic
- ¾ cup raisins (I like golden)
- 2 tsp. capers (I like a bit more myself.)
- 1 cup stuffed green olives each sliced 2 times.
- 1 8oz. can tomato sauce

Add to meat mixture, stir well, cover pan and cook for 15 minutes. Cool slightly, and thoroughly mix in 3 well-beaten eggs.

Fill the pumpkin with the meat mixture, packing firmly. Cover loosely with the pumpkin lid. Place in a shallow greased baking pan, and bake 1 hour at 350 degrees.

Cool 10 minutes and serve cut into wedges.

NOTE: You should bring it out to the table on your best platter for your guests to enjoy, and cut and serve it at the table. We like to give it a special place of honor by putting it on a raised cake plate lined with autumn leaves.

I like to start with some kind of appetizer with any "big" dinner, and this one is sooo easy, and a great favorite.

Parmesan Rounds

Cut a whole loaf of good quality white bread into 3 or 4 inch rounds with a muffin cutter.

In a medium bowl combine:
> 1 c. grated Parmesan
> 1 c. Mayonnaise (Best Foods / Helmans only for me!)
> 1 c. chopped green onions – mostly the green part.

Spread a bit of mixture to cover each round generously and broil until golden brown. (Watch carefully.)

Serve hot from oven and watch them disappear!

A favorite green salad is really all that is needed for

an accompaniment, but if you would like to add a green vegetable, some roasted asparagus would be delicious.

Pecan, Pear, and Gorgonzola Salad

In a small skillet over medium heat sauté ½ cup pecan halves in 2 Tbs. butter and 2 tsp. sugar till carmelized. Set aside to cool

Cut one pear (whatever is ripe or available at the time) into ½ inch chunks.

Crumble 4 oz. gorgonzola cheese into ¼ inch chunks.

For the dressing, whisk together in a small bowl;
> ¼ c. good olive oil
> 3 Tbsp. balsamic vinegar
> 1 tsp. Dijon mustard
> ½ tsp. sugar
> Salt and pepper to taste

In a large salad bowl toss above ingredients with 6-8 hands-full of mixed spring greens or any salad greens you prefer. Serve immediately

Conclude with any of the desserts below, or one of your own favorites. (How about an apple pie or tart tatin?)

A VALENTINE'S DAY FETE

We usually like to have some kind of festive dinner around February just to shake off the winter blues, be hospitable, and celebrate old friends or new ones. So why not take advantage of Valentine's Day…it's a good excuse to do something special.

Blue Cheese and Lemon Chicken

- 1 1/3 c. sour cream
- 6 ounces mild blue cheese crumbled.
- 1 Tbsp. grated lemon zest
- ¼ c. freshly squeezed lemon juice
- 3 Tbsp. minced fresh parsley
- ½ c. all purpose flour
- 2 tsp. dried rosemary, crumbled
- 1 tsp. salt
- 1 tsp. pepper
- 6 boneless chicken breasts. (I prefer with skin on.)
- 3 tbsp. butter
- 3 tbsp. olive oil

- 2 cups fresh bread crumbs
- ½ cup butter, melted
- ½ c. freshly grated Parmesan cheese

Preheat the oven to 350. Lightly butter a baking dish large enough to hold the chicken breasts in a single layer.

Stir together the sour cream, blue cheese, lemon zest, lemon juice, and parsley in a medium bowl and set aside. Combine the flour, rosemary, salt and pepper in a shallow dish and stir to mix. Dredge the chicken in the flour mixture, coating the breasts evenly and patting to remove excess flour.

Heat the butter and oil in a large skillet over medium-high heat until it is just starting to brown. Add the chicken and cook until browned, about 4 minutes per side. (Cook the chicken in batches if they don't easily fit in the skillet; the skillet should not be crowded.) Transfer the chicken to the baking dish, skin side up. Spread the blue cheese mixture evenly over the chicken.

Combine the bread crumbs, melted butter, and Parmesan cheese in a medium bowl and stir to mix. Sprinkle the bread crumb mixture over the chicken and bake until the topping is nicely browned and the chicken is cooked through, about 20 minutes. (Juices run clear when pierced in the thickest part with the tip of a knife.)

This dish unfailingly generates rave reviews. Enjoy!

NOTE: Serve this with a salad, a green vegetable, and my fabulous potato gratin, (recipe follows) and your guests will be putty in your hands. And of course, don't forget one of my awesome desserts.

Gratin Dauphinois Michele

Although this is a fantastic French concoction, we recently served it to a pastor and his wife from Switzerland and they said it was very typically Swiss and made them feel at home. Either way, I know you will love this, and make it again and again.

- 1 garlic clove
- 2 pounds baking potatoes, such as russets, peeled and very thinly sliced. (A mandoline comes in very handy for this.)
- 2 cups freshly grated Gruyere cheese. (About 6 oz.)
- 1 cup heavy cream
- Salt and pepper.

Preheat the oven to 350.

Thoroughly rub a shallow 6-cup porcelain gratin dish (oval is best) with the garlic.

Layer half of the potatoes in the dish, like fish scales. Sprinkle with half of the cheese and then half of the cream. Sprinkle with salt and pepper. Add another layer, using the rest of the ingredients.

Bake, uncovered, until the gratin is crisp and golden on top, and the potatoes are tender - from 50 to 60 minutes. Serve immediately.

A MIDSUMMER JUBILEE

Crustade de Coq au Vin

Well actually, this could be served ANY time – mid-summer, mid-winter, mid-anything. It is one of my favorite dishes ever and although it takes a little work and patience, is well worth the effort. Coq au vin (chicken in wine) is another classic French dish. (No Swiss has yet laid claim to it, at least in my experience.) I was sitting at a little bistro with Becky in Lyon, France, on a luscious summer evening in June of 2006, eating "real" crustade de coq au vin. I looked at Becky and said, "Yours is better!" (And it's true – what can I say?!)

- 12 pcs of cut-up chicken
- ½ lb. slab bacon, cut into small pieces
- 1 pkg. frozen pearl onions
- 1 ½ tbsp. all purpose flour
- A whole bottle (honest) of dry red wine (Something you like well enough to drink.)
- 1 ½ c. chicken stock
- 1 ½ tbsp. tomato paste
- 2 bay leaves
- ¾ tsp. dried basil
- 3 tbsp. butter
- 2 lbs. fresh large mushrooms, trimmed and cut into quarters
- Salt
- Frozen puff pastry

1. Cut larger chicken pieces in half
2. In a large Dutch oven (I love my cast iron one) cook bacon over medium heat until all the fat is rendered, and bacon is brown. Remove with slotted

spoon and drain on paper toweling.

3. Cook chicken in a single layer in bacon fat, turning occasionally until golden brown on all sides. Remove, and drain on paper toweling.

4. Add onions to drippings in pan and cook, covered, over medium heat, shaking the Dutch oven occasionally, until the onions are golden brown. Remove onions and (what else?) drain on paper toweling.

5. Stir flour into drippings, and cook, stirring constantly, 2 minutes. Whisk in wine and stock. Add tomato paste, and spices. Reduce and cook until thickened and lovely.

6. Meanwhile, sauté mushrooms in butter (don't overcrowd!) until golden.

7. Combine mushrooms with sauce, onions, bacon, and chicken together in Dutch oven and cover with pastry. Bake at 350 for approximately 30 minutes, or until chicken is bubbly, and crust is golden brown.

Variation – if you would like to serve the coq over wide buttered noodles, you can omit the "crustade" (crust) and just bake covered with lid. Otherwise, the crust serves in place of the noodles…both are great…I always have a hard time deciding which to do.

If you're serving wine, it's a good idea to use the same kind you cooked the chicken in.

Serve with a salad, some crusty French bread to help soak up the fabulous juices, (if you're not doing noodles) and of course a wonderful dessert.

FOUR DESSERTS FOR ANY OCCASION

Mom's Cheesecake
This is not your regular cheesecake. It is a very old recipe – my mom used to make it all the time – and everyone who eats it says "Wow, this is absolutely delicious, and different from any cheesecake I've ever had."

For the crust: Pulverize almost a whole box of Vanilla Wafers in a food processor. (I keep out about 12 or so...otherwise it just seems to be too much.) If you don't have a food processor just crush them in a plastic bag with something heavy. Then mix the crumbs with 1½ sticks melted butter. Put the crumbs into a glass pie pan and press into sides and bottom to create a uniform crust.

Mix together in a food processor until creamy and smooth:
- 2 eggs
- ½ c. sugar.
- 1- 8 oz. and1–3 oz. pkg. of Philadelphia cream cheese.

Pour mixture into vanilla wafer crust and bake at 325 degrees for 25 minutes.
Remove from oven and cool. Meanwhile...
Mix together:

- 1 c. sour cream. (I use a few tbs. extra.)
- 3 tbs. sugar.
- 1 tsp. vanilla.

Pour over the cooked mixture in the pie crust and smooth the top. Return to the oven and bake for 8 minutes.

Remove from the oven, cool, then chill in the fridge.

NOTE: It's best to make this fairly early in the morning so it has the whole day to chill. Otherwise it might not be firm enough. Better yet, you can make it a day ahead if you like, just to be sure.

Kathryn's Key Lime Pie

Kathryn was a dear friend from church who grew up in Florida where key lime pie is king. This is her recipe, and it is so easy as to be ridiculous...but it is ridiculously delicious.
Mix in a food processor until smooth:

- ¾ c. *fresh* lime juice.
- 1 can sweetened, condensed milk
- 1- 8 oz. cream cheese, softened.

- 1 tsp. vanilla
- Zest of two limes.

Pour into a store-bought vanilla wafer or graham cracker crust. Refrigerate 3-4 hours or until firm. Serve with a dollop of whipped cream, and a paper-thin slice of lime for garnish.

NOTE: At first glance, this doesn't sound all that spectacular, but once you try it, you'll be sooo glad you didn't dismiss it as a bad idea.

Bardy Road Lemon Mousse

For a year and a half we were care-takers/givers at a beautiful home on a hilltop in Santa Rosa, with a spectacular view of rolling hills and vineyards. At the "Bardy Road" house, we grew lemons, and they provided the main ingredient for this scrumptious mousse.

- 1 ½ envelopes unflavored gelatin
- ½ cup water
- 1 tbsp. grated lemon zest
- ¾ c. freshly squeezed lemon juice
- 6 eggs
- 1 ½ c sugar
- ¼ tsp. salt
- 2 c. whipping cream

- 1 tsp. vanilla
- 2 tbsp. sugar.

In a small sauce pan, soak gelatin in water 5 minutes, then place over lowest heat until thoroughly dissolved.

Combine with lemon zest and juice.

Place eggs, sugar and salt in the bowl of a stand mixer (if you have one…a hand mixer will work if necessary) and beat at high speed until mixture is very thick and light, about 10 minutes. (It really takes that long, but it turns out beautifully!)

With beater at low speed, slowly add gelatin mixture. Chill until mixture begins to jell. (About 20 minutes.)

Whip one cup of the cream until it forms soft mounds, then fold into the gelatin-egg mixture. Pour into individual serving dishes…I like to use a small wine glass, and chill till ready to serve. (At least 30 minutes…more is better.)

Becky's Strawberry Devonshire Tort
I have friends that will practically kill for this dessert. Make sure you make enough!

Place a Pillsbury refrigerated pie crust (the kind you un-roll) into a removable-bottom tart pan, prick all over with a fork to help it stay flat, and bake until just golden brown.

Filling:
- 1 – 8 oz. pkg. cream cheese softened.
- 3 tbsp. sour cream

Beat cream cheese until fluffy, add sour cream, and beat until smooth.

Spread on bottom of cooled pie shell and refrigerate.

Wash and hull 2 qts. fresh strawberries.

Mash enough uneven berries to make 1 cup.

Force mashed berries through a sieve, and add water to make 1 cup.

Mix:
- 1 c. sugar
- 3 tbsp. cornstarch
- ½ c. water
- Sieved berries

Cook over medium heat, stirring, until mixture is clear and thickened, then boil about one minute.

Stir to cool slightly, and add a little red food coloring. (Just a few drops works great.)

Fill pie shell with remaining whole berries, arranged con-centrically with tips up, then pour cooked juice mixture over top as a glaze.

Chill at least one hour.

ACKNOWLEDGMENTS

With deepest love and gratitude I want to acknowledge the invaluable contribution of the team around me that gave steady encouragement, thoughtful advocacy, and wise counsel in writing this book; especially my dearest beloved Becky, as well as Adam Peacocke, Jason Deslongchamp, Clint and Tracy Davis, and Paul and Rheanna Smith. Thanks for your hospitable hearts.

ABOUT THE AUTHOR

Mike Dietrich graduated with a degree in history from Westmont College in Santa Barbara, California where he grew up. He is best friends with his wife; unashamedly proud of his two sons; fascinated, bewildered, and in love with his seven grandchildren. His other passions include serving as a pastor, mentor, discipler and bible teacher; conversing with friends and strangers; hosting convivial feasts; and pursuing a more intimate relationship with his hero, Jesus.

Mike can be reached at
michaelbeckyd@gmail.com

INVITED HOME

22196985R00143

Made in the USA
Lexington, KY
16 April 2013